How To Be A

WEEKEND ENTREPRENEUR

Making Money At Craft Fairs and Trade Shows

Susan Ratliff

Marketing Methods Press
Phoenix, Arizona

Library of Congress Catalog Card Number: 91-061415

ISBN 0-9624798-2-9

Author, Susan Ratliff
Illustrator, Sally Valentine

Printed in the United States of America

To Garrison Weller Ratliff, whose birth was my inspiration for becoming a weekend entrepreneur and to my husband, Steven, whose emotional support and willingness to manage the household on weekends, provided the opportunity for my success.

Acknowledgements

I have always maintained that enthusiasm can compensate for experience. It must have been my enthusiasm that convinced the publisher to take a chance on a first-time author.

My sincere appreciation goes to Barbara Lambesis for her support and confidence in my ability to write this book. Also, for the many hours she devoted to editing, revising and consulting that pulled it all together. Lori Yoney provided outstanding production support that helped keep the project on time.

I am grateful to Dr. John D. Ratliff and Marilyn Brady for their editing and proofreading assistance, to Sally Valentine for the wonderful illustrations and to Cindy Mackey for the terrific cover design.

A special thank you to my friends on the craft fair circuit and to the members of the Entrepreneurial Mothers Association and the Scottsdale Chamber of Commerce who have supported my business, shared information and encouraged this project.

TABLE OF CONTENTS

Starting a business ● Turn your creations into cash ● You don't have to make it yourself ● Making money with multi-level consumer products ● Selling a service ● Getting started ● Cashing in on craft fairs ● The retail trade show ● Specialty vendor carts ● Craft malls ● Wholesale trade shows ● Swap meets ● Opportunities are everywhere.

Planning for success ● Show dynamics ● The short-cut method.

Customer traffic is essential ● Will your customers be there? ● Location, location, location ● Operating days and hours ● Track record of the show promoter ● Competing for customers ● Exhibitor entry fees ● Drawing customers to the show ● Elements of successful shows ● Exhibitor's evaluation forms.

Publications listing craft fairs, trade shows and swap meets.

Your exhibit space ● The show schedule ● Staffing your exhibit ● Work requirements ● Collecting the cash ● Sharing space ● Exhibit security ● Set goals for every show ● Exhibitor etiquette.

Entry fees ● Book events early ● Jury procedures ● Getting accepted ● If rejected, don't give up ● Guidelines for getting accepted into the best shows.

INTRODUCTION

Inspiration and motivation are essential for success--especially when it comes to launching a business. Being inspired and motivated, however, isn't enough. Today, you must have knowledge to succeed. That's why learning basic business principles is absolutely necessary for anyone whose goals include becoming one's own boss, expanding an existing business venture or simply earning additional income with a small, home-based business. Being a successful weekend entrepreneur means using inspiration, motivation and knowledge to reach your goals.

Knowledge is power, and the power to achieve financial independence through exhibit marketing is outlined in this book. The instructions, techniques and skills necessary to build a successful, profitable weekend enterprise are explained in step-by-step detail. Whether you're a beginner or a seasoned veteran at exhibit marketing, the information contained in this handbook will help you make more money exhibiting and selling your goods and services at trade shows, craft fairs, swap meets and other weekend events.

Eleanor Roosevelt once said, "The future belongs to those who believe in the beauty of their dreams." Many people talk about their goals and dreams, but few actually attempt to fulfill them. If your dream is to develop a profitable weekend business, I hope this book provides the motivation and the "know how" you need to take the risk to jump in and try your luck.

If I can be a successful weekend entrepreneur, you can, too. Until I did it myself, I doubted anyone could make serious money with a weekend business. I never would have discovered this opportunity, if life changing events had not redirected my priorities.

Before I became a weekend entrepreneur, I enjoyed a successful sales and marketing career, first in the health spa industry and then in residential real estate. I loved my career and never considered doing anything else. However, like many career women without children, I became concerned about starting a family after my 33rd birthday. My husband and I decided it was time to have a baby. After I became pregnant, I continued to work full time, while making arrangements with clients to schedule business around my delivery date. I carefully planned a short, 60-day maternity leave--just enough time to adjust to motherhood, then get back to business without losing momentum.

The baby arrived and everything was perfect. Yet, as the end of the sixty days approached, I realized my priorities had changed dramatically. I decided to put my career on hold to give time and attention exclusively to my new baby.

As the months passed, however, I began to miss friends at the office. I longed for adult conversation and I craved the personal satisfaction that comes from accomplishing projects and making money. Even so, I still did not want to leave my son in the care of anyone else to return to a demanding 50-hour work week. That prompted me to begin looking for a business opportunity I could operate from my home.

Researching through business magazines, I discovered an opportunity that immediately got my attention -- personalized children's books. The idea was innovative and appealed to my new interests as a mother. The company, Premier Personalized Publishing, 670 International Parkway #120, Richardson, Texas 75081, (214) 231-3598, offered distributors the right to market different versions of hard cover, full-color books that featured the purchaser's favorite child as the star of the story and included the age, hometown, family and friends of the child, throughout the text, as well. The books were computer generated and could be produced in only four minutes, while the customer watched. The product line appeared to be the perfect vehicle for my sales and marketing background, so I purchased a distributorship. Unlike a franchise, a distributorship requires no percentage of sales and no payment of royalties. Distributors usually pay a one-time licensing fee and purchase supplies from the parent company.

I decided to sell the books at local craft fairs, since the fairs were scheduled on weekends, allowing me to spend weekdays with my son. When I worked Saturday and Sunday, my husband took over the parenting duties.

On October 7, 1988, I took two folding tables, two blue table cloths, my equipment and books and set up a display at my first craft fair. To my delight, I sold nearly $1,000 of merchandise that weekend. The business was off and running. That December I rented a vendor's cart at a local shopping mall to attract holiday shoppers. The business earned more than $19,000 in revenue in the first three months.

Since becoming a weekend entrepreneur, my business has grown steadily each year. In addition, I have remained one of the top four distributors in the nation for Premier Personalized Publishing. I succeeded by marketing my products at craft fairs, trade shows, weekend events and through shopping mall cart programs. I do not advertise with major media, but I do rely on my satisfied customers for repeat and referral business by utilizing a mailing list of more than 4,000 customers.

Anyone can build a successful business exhibit marketing, just like I did, by following the guidelines in this book. Making and selling your own products is one way to do it. Establishing a service business and promoting it at weekend events is another. In addition, many

3

inexpensive, money-making distributorships and franchises are available that are perfect for anyone seeking to establish a weekend enterprise without having to start from scratch. Don't wait any longer. Develop an idea of your own or look for new, unusual products and services that you can sell through exhibit marketing. Some ideas are listed below.

PRODUCTS: gift baskets, laser photo sculptures, balloon wrapped gifts, child identification cards, buttons and badges, monogrammed items, custom license plates, personalized bumper stickers, name bracelets, photo business cards, ceramic photo plates, computer portraits, instant old-time photos, instant engraving, fresh herb farming, personalized key chains, **PVC** furniture, dried flower arrangements, silk plants, custom closet designs, pencil embossing, talking balloons, removable tattoos, rubber stamps, instant novelty photos, gold by the inch, mini donuts, personalized calligraphy, hand puppets, handmade writing papers, mystery grab bags, photo buttons, balloon sculptures, pet photos, instant signs.

SERVICES: videotape services, gold stamping, desktop publishing, computerized diets, photography, auto detailing, janitorial services, house sitting, dating services, personal shopper, nanny placement, face painting, mobile bookkeeping, plant care services, laminating services, seminar promoting, delivery services, image consulting, financial planning, entertainment broker, palm reader, mortgage reduction services, self-defense training, event planning, laser cartridge recharging, computer programming, sculptured nails.

While building a weekend business, everyone will confront many challenges, as well as realize many rewards. Making money may be the primary reason for starting a weekend business, but other benefits and incentives also can be derived from the experience. I sometimes think the personal satisfaction I gain from overcoming obstacles, improving my business acumen and receiving admiration and respect from my peers is worth more than money. In 1989, I was honored as Arizona's Entrepreneurial Mother of the Year, an award presented by the Entrepreneurial Mothers Association. The public recognition and exposure generated by that award increased my personal self-confidence and improved my business credibility.

I have succeeded as a weekend entrepreneur because I love what I do. I am happy to share my successful experiences and knowledge with organizations and groups through the presentation of informative workshops and seminars on how to become a weekend entrepreneur using the profitable techniques of exhibit marketing.

For information, write to the address below.

Susan Ratliff
About Me! of Arizona
8100 E. Camelback, Suite 79
Scottsdale, Arizona 85251

CHAPTER 1

MAKING MONEY AS A
WEEKEND ENTREPRENEUR

Anyone can make money as a weekend entrepreneur by applying the proven techniques of exhibit marketing. Thousands of craft fairs, trade shows, and swap meets are held every year, most taking place on weekends. In addition, there are thousands of other events and hundreds of locations where enterprising people can exhibit and sell goods and services. These opportunities offer exhibitors the chance to make hundreds of dollars every weekend. Information in this book will explain the art of exhibit marketing and help you become successful at your very own money-making venture.

Exhibit marketing started hundreds of years ago at bazaars and open markets where people gathered to buy and sell food and merchandise. Today, craft fairs, trade shows and swap meets have evolved from simple neighborhood fundraisers to a sophisticated circuit of marketing outlets that showcase 50 to 800 exhibitors per event and draw as many as 15,000 shoppers. Making money in this lucrative marketplace is the goal of every weekend entrepreneur.

Starting A Business

Now is the time to start a weekend enterprise. Interest in small business ownership is surging and the number of new business start-ups continues to grow year after year. Help is readily available, since many public and non-profit organizations now offer free educational materials and individual counseling to anyone seeking assistance with a new business venture. Today's home-based business owner enjoys renewed respect, support and encouragement. In addition, many economic development agencies are placing special emphasis on helping women and minorities get started in business. There is no better time than the present to launch a business venture, since chances for success have never been greater with today's business climate favoring the development of small enterprises.

Weekend entrepreneurs get started for many reasons. Some want to start a business and keep the security of a full-time job, thus hedging their financial risk until they can become completely self-employed. Others want to stay home with their children, but still earn an income. And finally, some want to enjoy retirement, yet keep busy and earn extra money. Whatever the reason, people of many backgrounds with diverse goals have found exhibiting and selling at craft fairs, trade shows and swap meets rewarding.

Weekend entrepreneurs can earn from a few hundred dollars to as much as several thousand dollars every weekend by participating in successful craft fairs or trade shows. Weekend entrepreneurs also have the freedom to set their own work schedules according to their business goals and personal needs. Your success at exhibit marketing will depend on your desire to learn the skills necessary to do it right, and the amount of time you wish to devote to your new business.

Opportunities abound for anyone wishing to become a weekend entrepreneur. The talented artist or crafter who designs and produces unique creations, the smart salesperson who represents and markets products made by others, the multi-level marketer of consumer goods or the owner of a service business can benefit from exhibit marketing. Each entrepreneur offers something different, yet all can make money exhibiting and selling at craft fairs, trade shows, swap meets and other events on weekends.

Turn Your Creations Into Cash

Do you have a hobby or a special creative talent? Marketing what you design and manufacture is one way to begin a weekend business. A person with a sewing hobby, for example, could make and sell pillows, comforters or quilts. Hand-sewn dolls and stuffed animals of all varieties always sell briskly at craft fairs. One successful seamstress sews monograms on aprons and sports towels. She brings her sewing machine to every show and produces her work on site. Customers enjoy watching her customize their purchases and she loves taking home a purse full of cash.

Interested in jewelry? Most craft fairs and trade shows have vendors selling beautiful, fine gold and silver jewelry made by professional gold and silversmiths. In addition, less expensive, unusual costume jewelry also is a hit at these events. Earrings made of paper, necklaces fashioned from bandanas and ceramic bracelets are just a few examples of creative costume jewelry that sell well at fairs. One innovative entrepreneur designs, paints and sells necklaces with matching earrings made from cookie dough.

If your creative talents are limited, consider what some enterprising people are doing with simple T-shirts. Decorated T-shirts remain consistent best sellers at craft fairs and trade shows. With a little practice, anyone can attractively trim T-shirts with ribbons, sequins or appliques. Painted T-shirts also are very fashionable. While some are beautifully decorated with detailed artwork, others are simply spray painted or spun on a wheel and splattered with paint to produce an appealing, popular product. Ideas for creating interesting and desirable T-shirts seem endless.

Woodworking skills can payoff at weekend events, too. Talented persons who carve duck decoys, animals or children's toys and exhibit them have no trouble finding buyers for their products. Anyone skilled with a jigsaw can produce puzzles in animal shapes or cut names from solid blocks of wood. Custom wooden signs with sayings like "The Ratliff Family" or "Steven's Room" are popular and can be made on the spot using woodburning equipment. Swings, rockers, stools, curio shelves and other wooden furniture and accessories appeal to craft fair and trade show shoppers.

Whether you turn an existing hobby into a business or start from scratch by developing a new item to market, if you design, create or produce anything, chances are, you can sell it and make money at weekend events.

You Don't Have To Make It Yourself

You don't have to possess creative talents or even manufacture products to be a successful weekend entrepreneur. Almost anyone can build a business selling merchandise made by others. Many ways exist to assemble an impressive product inventory. Once you select and acquire the merchandise, use successful exhibiting skills to make money by selling the goods at weekend events.

With this approach, the first step is to decide on a merchandising theme. What type of items will comprise your product line and where will you find them? For example, a business that decides to sell country-style items should look for shows attended by manufacturers of country-style products. By talking to exhibitors selling country crafts, it's possible to find those willing to let someone else sell their products. Many talented artisans would gladly give up marketing their work, if they could find a competent entrepreneur to do it for them.

Other sources of inventory can be found at wholesale trade shows, where hundreds of manufacturers seek representatives to market different products. Resourceful merchants also explore auctions, factory close-outs, business bankruptcies, and manufacturer's samples to acquire inventory. These sources provide opportunities to purchase reasonable quantities of merchandise at terrific discounts. Clothing, household gadgets, sunglasses, cosmetics and many other items can be acquired from these sources.

Inventory can be purchased or taken on consignment. Purchasing inventory creates business assets, but also ties up hundreds of dollars.

Until things start selling, cash flow can be a problem. Therefore, when possible, you may wish to acquire some or all of your inventory on consignment. This means receiving merchandise, free of charge, and paying the producer a prearranged price only when the merchandise is sold. It is possible to build an impressive product line with consignment items, and receive as much as 40 to 60 percent of the retail price when the items are sold.

Making Money With Multi-level Consumer Products

Multi-level marketing of basic consumer products has produced many millionaires. Most Americans have heard of Shaklee, Mary Kay, and Amway. Products distributed by these companies are sold through network marketing by a multi-level sales force. Thousands of products and services provided by hundreds of companies are sold through this method, creating lucrative, part-time business opportunities for many. The entrepreneur who becomes involved in a multi-level company makes a small investment for start-up products and sales training. Then, the individual starts selling the products, while recruiting others to do the same. Success is achieved in multi-level marketing when entrepreneurs are able to build a network of sales representatives who work under them, since recruiters get a sales commission on everything sold by members of their network.

Trade show exhibiting is ideal for individuals with a multi-level business, because it provides the opportunity to sell products direct to the public, as well as recruit new sales representatives. Shows that offer a demonstration area are ideal for making professional presentations and provide excellent exposure for the multi-level marketer. Information about companies offering business opportunities in multi-level or network marketing can be found in magazines like *Entrepreneur, Business Opportunities* and *Success.*

Selling A Service

Service businesses can be promoted successfully at craft fairs and trade shows, as well. Face-painting, computer horoscopes, photography, and sculptured nails are some of the service businesses making money at weekend events. When a service business exhibits at a show or fair, often the goal is to acquire solid customer leads which will be followed by a sales call at a later date. Individuals involved in consumer service businesses should consider exhibit marketing on the weekends as a means to expand their businesses and acquire new customers. Chiropractors, financial planners, carpet cleaners, landscapers and many other service business owners have successfully promoted their companies at weekend events.

Getting Started

The techniques of successful exhibit marketing are explained in this book. Everything you need to know to get started with a weekend enterprise is contained between these covers. While craft fairs, retail trade shows and swap meets will be referenced most often throughout the book, other new and innovative marketing possibilities where exhibit marketing techniques can be used also are explored. Not every alternative event will be suitable for your line of products or services, nevertheless you should make yourself aware of every opportunity available to make money with your newly acquired knowledge and skills.

Cashing In On Craft Fairs

The craft fair also is known as a boutique, bazaar, arts and crafts fair, or festival. Several varieties exist, ranging from small, local fairs to large events scheduled on the national craft fair circuit. The best place for a beginner to start exhibiting is at small, local craft fairs and events.

Schools, churches, shopping centers and private residences are the locations of most local fairs. These events feature 20 to 100 vendors, and can attract as many as 3,000 shoppers to a three-day weekend event. Usually, the atmosphere at a local fair is casual and a diverse line of merchandise and services is displayed. Few restrictions apply for entering local fairs. Therefore, shoppers find everything from hand-woven clothing to spin-art T-shirts, finely tooled decoys to rustic country carvings, hair bows to doll clothes, cinnamon rolls to Mexican tamales being sold at local fairs.

These events often are held outdoors, making the atmosphere at the local craft fair fun, friendly and informal. When put in a festive mood by the atmosphere, shoppers spend freely and are easy to approach and engage in conversation. Craft fair shoppers buy gifts, decorator items, personal attire, functional products and holiday decorations. They expect quality and uniqueness in the items they purchase, and they want them at a reasonable price. The local craft fair is the ideal starting place for a beginner to learn exhibit marketing and continues to be the mainstay for many seasoned exhibitors. If your products or services appeal to people who frequent craft fairs, local events in your area are great places to start your new business venture.

When success is achieved on the local circuit, the more serious entrepreneurs, artists and crafters progress to the larger fairs. Many of the larger fairs are part of the national craft fair circuit that travels to major cities across the country. Most of the same sales and marketing techniques described later in this book will apply to both local and national fairs, but the entry requirements for the high profile events are more restrictive. At the large, national craft fairs, fine quality and excellent craftsmanship are demanded of the products sold by participating vendors. Only hand-crafted works and fine art are permitted at these fairs. Usually, vendors also are expected to submit their works to a jury, a judging committee, for approval before being accepted as a show vendor. National craft fairs feature exhibits by sculptors, portrait artists, silversmiths, photographers and other artists and craftspeople. These fairs cater to a more sophisticated shopper, one who is willing to pay a premium price for quality artwork and who is not necessarily looking for bargains.

The Retail Trade Show

Retail trade shows, not to be confused with wholesale trade shows, can offer enormous exposure for both a weekend and a full-time business. Sometimes called expos, gift marts, or exhibitions, these events are organized by professional show promoters. Retail trade shows usually are held at convention centers, hotels and fairgrounds, and are open to the buying public.

Retail trade shows feature products that revolve around a common theme, such as bridal accessories and services; home and garden products; office equipment, supplies and services; baby items; or recreation and sporting goods. Some shows have general themes that encompass many products and services, such as franchise opportunities, women-owned businesses or service companies. Entry requirements for retail trade shows are minimal, so a wide variety of products and services are exhibited at these events.

The key to successful exhibit marketing at retail trade shows is careful selection of shows. Exhibit only at those that will attract buyers interested in the products or services you offer. If you sell something that either fits the theme of the event or appeals to the expected audience, renting space and exhibiting at the show probably will be profitable.

Retail trade shows differ from craft fairs in several ways. First, the atmosphere at a retail trade show is more professional and business-like than the atmosphere at a backyard craft fair. Second, the type of customer attending usually has been carefully targeted by the promoter, so vendors have a clear idea of who will attend. Third, the shows are larger. As many as 200 to 500 exhibitors are featured at a retail trade show, and it is not unusual to have 3,000 to 10,000 people attend the show during a weekend.

Retail trade shows also offer an effective way to introduce a new product or gather information for new product development. In addition, exhibitors can expand their marketing reach nationwide by exposing their products and services to other exhibitors attending these shows from all over the country.

When vendors have perfected their exhibiting skills and are confident of their selling abilities, they can try some other money-making, exhibit marketing opportunities. Many marketing outlets including vendor carts, craft malls and wholesale trade shows offer excellent selling opportunities.

Specialty Vendor Carts

One new merchandising outlet is the specialty vendor cart, available for rent at most major shopping malls. These portable retail units are constructed to look like old-fashioned street vendors' carts and provide maximum exposure to mall traffic. These carts offer a festive presentation for unique products with broad appeal and can promote impulse buying from customers. Vendors selling from these carts offer everything from trendy accessories and gifts to traditional items and souvenirs. Products that are not readily available and do not compete with merchandise sold by other mall merchants are ideal for vendor carts. Products like personalized items, children's books, packaged food items, license plates and signs, gift baskets, baby items, tourist clothing, gifts, baseball cards and jewelry sell easily from vendor carts.

Vendor carts appeal to small business owners because they can be rented for short time periods. A rental commitment can be as short as 30 days. Rental rates range from $200 to $500 a week during the off season and from $300 to $1000 a week during the prime holiday season. A percentage of  the vendor's gross sales, usually 10% to 20%, also must be paid to the mall after sales reach a certain point.

Vendors with the right products and who are able to rent several carts at different locations during the prime selling months from October to December, can use this marketing vehicle to rapidly expand a business by hiring staff to operate them. Check with mall managers about cart rental programs. Most will have information packets available for business owners interested in vendor cart rentals.

Craft Malls

Craft malls are one of the hottest new marketing concepts available to artists and crafters. They are sprouting up everywhere, because the concept is simple and effective. The craft mall provides a place where weekend entrepreneurs can expand their businesses by displaying and selling their goods at a permanent location. Crafters and artists are free to concentrate on production or to exhibit at other fairs and shows.

The first crafter's mall, Coomer's, was founded by three businessmen in Ft. Worth, Texas in 1988. Coomer's now operates the largest chain of crafter's malls in the Southwest and plans to expand its chain nationwide. In addition, many similar facilities are opening all over the country, providing crafters with low-cost, permanent outlets for their products.

Craft malls are located in large buildings or set up in tents as outdoor markets. Some are open only weekends, while others stay open seven days a week. Vendors rent space, in various sizes, for one month or several months. Then, they set up their displays, price their merchandise as desired and keep their inventory well-stocked. The mall staff does the rest. They sell the merchandise, track the inventory by computer and take special orders. They pay the sales tax, utility bills and advertising. No commissions are requested and vendors get paid every two weeks for all items sold. Craft malls are a hassle-free way to have a storefront location without having enormous overhead.

Wholesale Trade Shows

Wholesale trade shows are designed to introduce producers or manufacturers of products to retail store owners and manufacturer's representatives. Store owners order products at wholesale prices and sell them to the public at retail prices. Manufacturer's representatives contract with producers to represent and sell products to retailers on commission. Buyers and sellers do all their business by purchase orders. Products are ordered at the show, but delivered and paid for at a later date. No money changes hands at the show and product samples are not permitted to leave the sales floor. Wholesale trade shows are closed to the public. Only business owners, product representatives and qualified buyers may attend.

People from all over the country attend wholesale trade shows, making these events exciting and energizing. One large order obtained at one of these shows could turn a weekend business into a national enterprise. Proper preparation, however, is essential when attempting to do business as an exhibitor in the wholesale marketplace.

For example, if a chain of children's stores places an order for 2,000 pairs of your painted baby shoes, could you fill the order? How long would it take to produce and ship them? What type of volume discount would you offer? To be successful at wholesale trade shows, vendors who manufacture goods or represent the products of other companies must understand requisites like manufacturing capacity, production schedules and shipping requirements and be prepared to answer customer's questions.

While most weekend entrepreneurs will never venture into the wholesale marketplace, those wishing to pursue this marketing avenue should take some sound advice--acquire a year or two of exhibiting and business experience, and fine tune your production process before attempting to exhibit and sell at wholesale trade shows.

Swap Meets

Another new outlet for exhibit marketers is indoor swap meets, operated by companies like Festival Markets Inc., of Las Vegas, which has several facilities in the Southwest. Buildings housing indoor swap meets can be as large as 130,000 square feet, providing space for as many as 700 vendors. A standard space rents for approximately $250 for a four-week period that includes 12 selling days. All vendors must carry new merchandise, which distinguishes this concept from other swap meets which usually are held outdoors with vendors dealing in both new and used merchandise.

Swap meets draw thousands of people looking for bargains and a day of entertainment. Almost every community has at least one permanet swap meet location.

Opportunities Are Everywhere

A list of other locations and events that have money making potential follows. These events can provide excellent selling opportunities for both the seasoned exhibitor and the beginner; entrepreneurs who are able to match their products with the purposes and themes of the events and the audiences they are likely to attract.

Antique Shows	Swap Meets
Grand Openings	Sporting Events
Balloon Festivals	Celebrations
Conventions	Shopping Malls
Rodeos	Car Shows
Baby Fairs	Wine Tastings
Carnivals	State and County Fairs
Parenting Groups	Church Events
Auctions	Charity Events
Gift Shows	Corporate Parties
Block Parties	Air Shows
Flea Markets	School Functions

Opportunities to show and sell products and services are everywhere. The resourceful weekend entrepreneur always will be on the lookout for places to apply exhibit marketing skills.

CHAPTER 2

THE CRAFT FAIR, TRADE SHOW & SWAP MEET CIRCUIT

Most weekend entrepreneurs start their new business ventures slowly. Most have limited time and money to invest, so care must be taken to understand how the craft fair and trade show circuit works before taking the plunge and attempting to sell products or services at these events. If you are patient enough to plan in advance, you can save yourself both time and money. Solid preparation and some early information gathering can help guarantee your weekend business will be successful. Start by visiting shows and fairs to get a feel for how exhibit marketing works.

Planning For Success

First, make a list of all of the shows, fairs and meets that are available in your area. Study the list, then select a few events in the immediate future that will be convenient for you to attend.

Visit as many shows as possible. Attend as a shopper, and take along a pencil and paper so you can make notes. Later, you can compare your observations with the elements of the perfect show detailed in chapter three and the information about displays, promotion and sales techniques described later in this book. This look and learn method of compiling preliminary information is essential for making sound business decisions. It will help you get your new enterprise off the ground and see that it is built on a strong foundation of knowledge.

Show Dynamics

When visiting each event, look at all the dynamics that surround exhibit marketing. Observe the customer traffic patterns and ask yourself the following questions. Is there a constant flow of people coming into the show? Is there a line of customers waiting at the check-out counter to buy merchandise? Does the show seem crowded to you? Is the atmosphere lively and pleasant? Are people buying or just looking?

Study the characteristics of the crowd. What type of people are attending? Are they mostly women, men, mothers with small children, senior citizens or employees on their lunch hour? Do most meet your customer profile? Are these people likely to purchase the type of products you intend to sell?

Examine the merchandise offered by exhibitors. Would your products complement the show or fit in with the theme? Is the quality of the merchandise displayed comparable to the quality of your offerings? Does the general atmosphere encourage sales? Does the show appear to be professionally run? Does the promoter attempt to meet the needs of the exhibitors?

Look carefully at all the displays and note the effectiveness of each. What is the overall image of the show? How are the displays constructed? What props are being used? Which booths seem the busiest? Would the setting be appropriate for displaying your products? Make notes and list any ideas you would like to incorporate into your exhibit.

Count the number of direct competitors exhibiting at each location. Study their displays and examine how they have arranged their products in their display space. Listen to their sales presentation. Evaluate their merchandise.

Observe the exhibitors in general. When they are not busy with a sale, ask vendors if they are having a good show. Tell them you are considering a space in the next one and would like their recommendations. Would they exhibit at the show again? What is their attitude toward the promoter, location and people attending? Determine if the majority of exhibitors are motivated and positive, or negative and complaining.

Locate the promoter and introduce yourself. Provide some information about yourself and your emerging business. Give the promoter a business card and a brochure, if you have one. Ask to be placed on the promoter's exhibitor mailing list and to be notified of the next show.

When you get home, carefully evaluate your notes. Compare what you observed on your scouting mission with the elements of a successful show outlined in the next chapter. After visiting several fairs and shows, you should understand more clearly how they operate and be better equipped to determine if exhibit marketing is the right avenue for your products and the best way to develop your enterprise.

The Short Cut Method

Perhaps you're thinking you'd like to avoid doing the groundwork, like scouting shows in advance. You are anxious to get started making money, now! A word of caution may be in order. I skipped serious planning and evaluating when I started and I wasted time and money learning by trial and error. However, if you are determined to jump in and start exhibiting at shows without first attending some that seem suitable for your products, at least follow the short-cut method below to minimize major mistakes and assure a certain degree of success.

Read chapter three, so you will understand the elements that make shows successful and chapter four to discover where to find future craft fairs, trade shows and swap meets. You must plan your schedule and apply to each show at least three months prior to the event. After listing the shows you wish to apply to, contact the promoter by phone. Introduce yourself and mention you are interested in the possibility of exhibiting at the next show. Use the evaluation form at the end of chapter three to gather as much data as you can. Make your scheduling decisions based on the answers received from each promoter. Then, apply to the shows that seem to have the greatest potential for profit.

CHAPTER 3

SHOWS THAT MAKE MONEY

There are hundreds of craft fairs, trade shows and swap meets to choose from each season, some compete on the same weekend. Therefore, it is essential to select shows and fairs that will generate the most profit from the sale of your particular products. To be a successful weekend entrepreneur, concentrate initial efforts on learning everything you can about the craft fair and trade show circuit. Plan a successful business strategy. Pay attention to the details that will keep you from making costly mistakes and will put you on the road to success and profit quickly.

All shows are not equal, so before you pay an entry fee to exhibit, take time to study the factors that make some shows better than others. Understand the elements that must be present in order to minimize risk and maximize profits. When you can identify the elements of a successful show, you will feel more confident about picking those that will be the most profitable. Remember, the best shows are those in which the exhibitor accomplishes specific goals and goes home happy.

Customer Traffic Is Essential

The first and most important element necessary for successful exhibit marketing is customer traffic. Selling success is tied directly to how many people walk past an exhibit. Selling is a numbers game. The higher the number of people attending the show, the higher the potential for sales and profit. Unless enough buyers attend a craft fair or trade show at which you exhibit, none of your other sales and marketing efforts will matter. So, always look for events that will expose your products to the largest number of potential buyers at the lowest possible cost. This should be your primary consideration when determining which exhibiting opportunities to schedule. Show promoters understand the importance of informing exhibitors of customer traffic and previous sales figures when attempting to attract quality vendors. Most reputable and experienced promoters will have literature about their craft fair, trade show or swap meet available for interested exhibitors. This information usually includes attendance and sales figures from previous years. If the promoter cannot provide printed materials, ask if the information can be released verbally. Then, make an adjustment for slight exaggeration.

Will Your Customers Be There?

Show selection is easier when you know the characteristics of your typical customer. Clearly determine who is most likely to buy what you intend to sell, who wants or needs what you have to offer. These people are your potential customers, your specific type of buyer. Determine if they are likely to be mothers, grandparents, business managers, store owners, retirees, men, women or teenagers.

For example, the potential customer of the vendor who sells baby items will be a female parent or grandparent, most likely. Items with a dinosaur theme, probably will attract customers buying gifts for teenagers and children. Hand-tooled, leather briefcases will attract buyers with a business background. Gift baskets appeal to a wider audience, but are purchased most often by women.

Understanding your customer will help you achieve purposeful marketing and will maximize your selling efforts. The chances of making a sale increase substantially when seven out of ten people attending a show might need or want what you have to offer. Exhibitors who choose to ignore the importance of pinpointing their potential customers waste substantial time and money at shows that do not generate sales. So, analyze the characteristics of the customer most likely to purchase your products. Then, find out if the shows you are considering cater to these people. Do this before you send in your entry fee.

Location, Location, Location

The location of a show is a critical factor in determining where to exhibit. A good location is necessary for a successful craft fair or trade show. Money-making shows are held at a variety of different sites. Most craft fairs are outdoors, while the majority of trade shows are held indoors. Whether a show is staged in a huge tent, at a convention center, or in the middle of a public park, three important location factors have a bearing on the show's success, no matter where it is held.

The first factor is parking. There must be adequate and convenient parking available near the location to encourage lots of customers to attend. Nothing is more discouraging to a potential shopper than driving around for 10 minutes looking for a place to park, then walking five blocks to the entrance. If customers start thinking about carrying purchases several blocks and having to remember where they parked, there's a good chance they will not stop to attend the event.

The second factor is exposure. A great location must have good exposure. Determine if the show will have direct exposure to a major street. When people drive by and are able to see the festivities, many will be curious and will stop to see what's attracting the crowd. Excellent visibility from the street can double attendance with walk-in traffic. Smart promoters will make sure there are large, eye-catching signs at all the major, nearby intersections announcing the show and directing people to it.

The third factor is access. Determine if the event is centrally located, at a site that provides easy access. Having to travel a long distance to reach an event can discourage many potential shoppers from attending. Make certain the location is convenient for the majority of people the promoter hopes to attract.

Operating Days And Hours

Find out how many selling days are included in the price of the entry fee. There are one-day shows, three-day shows and one-week shows. You will find that exhibiting three days at a cost of $75 will usually net more profit than exhibiting only one day for a cost of $50.

Show hours also will have an impact on your success as an exhibitor. For example, if products are aimed at employed people, make sure the show opens early and closes late so customers can drop by before or after work. If the weather will be hot, determine if the show opens early enough for morning customers to beat the heat.

When several shows operate on the same day, competition can split attendance and undermine all the events. This conflict in scheduling could have a big impact on the number of people attending each show. The specific days of the week a show runs also has some impact on attendance. Craft fairs usually pull the most shoppers on Thursday, Friday and Saturday, while retail trade shows and swap meets do best on Saturday and Sunday.

Track Record Of The Show Promoter

The experience of the promoter can effect the success of a particular show. Look for shows with a proven track record. Shows that have operated for three or more years usually are the safest bet. Shows that repeat year after year often establish a strong customer following and offer a good mix of exhibitors. An established promoter usually has a customer mailing list used to advertise the event and generate repeat traffic. You can feel confident that most craft fairs and trade shows with a track record will run smoothly and have adequate attendance.

This doesn't mean you should always rule out a first year show.

Evaluate the other criteria mentioned to determine if a newly organized show has potential for your products.

It's always a good idea to ask how many exhibitors the show will include and how many vendors have exhibited in the past. Request the names and phone numbers of several past exhibitors and call them for recommendations and opinions about previous shows. If the number of exhibitors has steadily increased each year, you can assume the show is successful and the word has spread among vendors.

Several weeks before a show opens, ask how many exhibit spaces have been sold. If the show is expecting 200 exhibitors and 150 booths are sold, consider entering if the event targets your customers and the entry fee is affordable. If the show turns out to be a flop, at least you will have 150 bored exhibitors with nothing to do but walk around visiting booths. The clever exhibitor can make a profit, even at poorly attended shows, by selling merchandise to other exhibitors.

Competing For Customers

Do not be afraid of competition! Competition is healthy. When competitors exhibit in shows you are considering, it usually confirms that the products you intend to sell will appeal to the show's attendees. When you meet other vendors with products similar to yours, use the opportunity to learn from them and analyze their strengths and weaknesses. Compare your offerings with that of the competition for design, quality and special services like delivery, shipping or gift wrapping. Keep abreast of exactly what the competition is selling, then give the public something a bit different.

For example, consider decorated T-shirts. At least five different vendors will be selling T-shirts at any large craft fair or trade show. If you look carefully at each vendor's product, you'll notice that some vendors sell spin art T-shirts, some sell hand-painted designs, some offer appliqued styles and some sell T-shirts decorated with ribbon. The point is, each artist has found a different way to make their shirts unique, thus offering a variety of choices to appeal to differing customer tastes.

A very successful T-shirt vendor in Arizona is a woman who paints paper earrings to match her spin-art T-shirts. She sells a shirt and earrings as a set for $15. The cost to make the earrings is about one dollar, yet by adding the matching earrings the customer perceives the value of the earrings and T-shirt to be greater than the value of a T-shirt alone. This perception of greater value is the reason she sells more than twice as many T-shirts as the competition.

Do not be discouraged from entering a show that has direct competition. Just offer something different, or give your products a new twist. If possible, select a booth location far enough away from a competitor, so you are not within sight of one another.

If you still cringe at the thought of having direct competition at the same show, think about this: How many times have you driven down the street and passed by a McDonald's fast food restaurant on one corner and Burger King directly across the street? Each sells very similar products, at almost identical prices, in similar surroundings. So, why should these two corporate giants locate so close to one another? First, because market research probably showed there was plenty of business for both. Second, each one feeds off the aggressive advertising and promotional efforts of the other. And finally, they are marketing to a similar audience. Anyone driving by, in the mood for a burger, will pull into one restaurant or the other, depending on brand loyalty or convenience of location. The point is, there usually is plenty of business for everyone.

Exhibitor Entry Fees

Do not let a high-priced exhibitor's fee discourage you from entering a show that has all the elements necessary to be successful for your enterprise. When starting your venture, be cautious and select the smaller shows first. Then, work your way into the larger ones. As you become more established and gain experience, develop a budget that permits you to enter some of the larger events that attract thousands of shoppers. If entry fees are too high for you to afford alone, consider sharing space with another exhibitor whose products would complement yours. Always check with the promoter in advance to determine if booth sharing is permitted.

To operate a successful weekend enterprise, you must treat your venture as a serious business. That means developing a budget to include exhibitor's fees, cost of products, supplies and promotional expenses. Budgeting will be easier if you anticipate all the expenses associated with the average show. The local craft fair, put on by a promoter who resides in your community, usually charges an entry fee of $20 to $100 and will sometimes deduct a 10 to 15 percent commission from your gross sales receipts. A national craft fair, which travels on a circuit to major cities throughout the country, will charge between $200 and $500 for an exhibit space and doesn't take a commission on sales. Entry fees for the typical retail trade show vary between $300 to $1,500, with no commission taken by the promoter.

Drawing Customers To The Show

Advertising plays a key role in determining the success of a show. The more an event is promoted, the larger the crowd likely to attend. Ask the promoter how the event will be publicized to encourage people to attend.

Small, local shows usually have a limited budget for advertising. These shows are promoted most commonly by placing large, easy-to-read signs at the major intersections nearest the show's location on the days of the event. Most show operators also mail notices to customers who have attended previous shows. Another common practice is to require all the exhibitors to hand out flyers to their customers, family and friends, announcing the event several weeks before the show date.

Find out if the promoter has scheduled any paid media advertising. Advertising in the daily and weekly newspapers can give shows a big boost in attendance. Radio, TV and magazine advertising is absolutely essential to the success of large craft fairs, retail trade shows and new swap meets.

Large events also can attract sponsors, such as well-known corporations, or radio or TV stations. The sponsors, seeking visibility, often donate pre-event media coverage or funds for promotion in return for recognition as a sponsor. Charity affiliations also can increase customer traffic, as well as sales. Some shoppers are more apt to buy products at a show, if they know a portion of the proceeds from the sale will be donated to a worthwhile charity.

Occasionally, a fair is part of the activities offered at an annual community event or celebration. Even though the high traffic potential at these events is enticing, always evaluate whether the event will attract your specific potential customers and if the atmosphere is conducive for selling your products. Certain large events draw huge crowds, thousands of people. Nevertheless, because most of the activities are free, many families attending are looking for cheap entertainment, not things to buy.

Elements Of Successful Shows

When putting together a show schedule always evaluate the shows you are considering by the criteria outlined in this chapter to help you determine the potential for success at each event. If some elements are missing, but a show is strongly recommended by someone you know or you've heard good things about it, you may want to take the risk and try it anyway.

Fill out an evaluation form when scouting potential exhibiting opportunities in advance and after exhibiting at each show. Keep the forms on file and refer to them each season when planning your show schedule. Also, when it's not possible to visit the show in advance, use this form as a guide to question promoters by phone to determine the potential of an event.

Exhibitor's Evaluation Forms

A supply of 50 exhibitor evaluation forms similar to the ones that follow, but printed on 8 1/2" x 11" paper, are available from Marketing Methods Press. Send a check for $10, which includes shipping and handling, along with a request for Exhibitor Evaluation Forms to Marketing Methods Press, 1413 E. Marshall, Phoenix, AZ 85014 or call (602) 840-7308 to place a Visa or MasterCard order.

EXHIBITOR'S SHOW EVALUATION FORM

Show Name:_____ Theme:_____

Show Location:_____

Promoter's Name:_____Phone No:_____

Month:_____Days & Dates __M__T__W__TH__F__S__S

Hours:____Exhibitor's Fee $ ____Commission on sales_____%

Space Size:_____ Fee includes: table[ ] 6'[ ] 8'[ ] chair[ ]

Central Cashier: Y N   Juried: Y N

Booth sharing permitted: Y N

History: 1st-yr. show [ ] 2nd-yr. show [ ] 3 or more yrs. [ ]

No. of Shoppers Expected:_____Last Year's Attendance: _____

Number of Exhibits:_____Number of Competitors: _____

Average sales volume per exhibitor: $_____

Shopper Traffic: Crowded [ ] Busy [ ] Slow [ ] Dead [ ]

Primary Type of Shopper: Women [ ] Men [ ] Children [ ]
                    Teens [ ] Business people [ ] Seniors [ ]

Exhibitor Attitude: Positive [ ]   Negative [ ]   Indifferent [ ]

Atmosphere: Professional [ ]   Casual [ ]   Festive [ ]

Merchandise: Quality products [ ] Amateur [ ] Fits my theme [ ]

Parking: Close to entrance Y N   Adequate space   Y N

Access: Convenient Y N   Visible from the street Y N

Advertising: Newspaper [ ] Radio [ ] Sponsor [ ] Signs [ ] Mail [ ]

Exhibitor references:

Name_____Phone_____

Comments_____

Name_____Phone_____

Comments_____

Name_____Phone_____

Comments_____

CONCLUSIONS: Don't miss this one [ ] Possibility [ ] Skip it [ ]

Application requested: Y N   Application & fee sent on:_____

SHOW RESULTS

Total Cash Sales $_____ (excluding taxes)

Tax Collected $_____

Total Cash Collected $_____

Amount due from Promoter $_____ (total cash sales minus commission)

Amount received from Promoter $_____ Date received_____

Number of sales _____ Total leads collected _____

Number of special orders taken: _____Cash value of orders: $____

Number of new customers to add to mailing list:_____

EXPENSE LIST

Product costs (time and materials)	$_____
Exhibitor's fee	$_____
Commission to promoter	$_____
Show services	$_____
Transportation	$_____
Accommodations	$_____
Advertising/promos	$_____
Miscellaneous	$_____

TOTAL EXPENSES $_____

Cash Sales ($) minus Expenses ($) = Net Profit $_____

SHOW EVALUATION

Weather: Sunny [ ] Warm [ ] Cold [ ] Windy [ ] Rain [ ]

Space Location: Excellent [ ] Good [ ] Fair [ ] Poor [ ]

Comments:_____

Promoter's Services: Excellent [ ] Good [ ] Fair [ ] Poor [ ]

Comments:_____

Problems:_____

What to do differently next year: _____

_____

CONCLUSION: Sign up for next year [ ] Possibility [ ] Skip it [ ]

CHAPTER 4

FINDING EXHIBITING OPPORTUNITIES

Exhibiting opportunities are never hard to find. First, review the entertainment section and the calendar of events published in daily and weekly newspapers for listings of upcoming community activities and trade shows. In some communities swap meets and craft fairs also are advertised in the classified section of local newspapers.

Contact the local Chamber of Commerce, Civic Center, Convention Bureau or Center for the Arts to obtain a roster of future conventions, shows and events taking place in your area.

Ask other vendors about future exhibiting opportunities. Obtain leads at local shows. Many craft fair operators distribute flyers advertising future events at tables near the fair entrance. Moreover, individuals in many cities compile and sell listings of all the local craft fairs as a guide for exhibitors, as well as shoppers. Always look for places to exhibit your products and services and explore the list of resources that follow to help you locate craft fairs, trade shows and swap meets near you.

Listings Of Craft Fairs, Trade Shows & Swap Meets

The Crafts Report, 700 Orange Street, P.O. 1992, Wilmington, DE 19899-9962.

Sunshine Artists USA, 1700 West Sunset Drive, Longwood, Florida 32750-9697.

Harris Rhodes Show List, P.O. Box 142-L, LaVeta, Colorado 81055. (719) 742-3146

Where It's At, George T. Jones, 7204 Bucknell Drive, Austin, Texas 78723. (512) 926-7954

Craftmaster News, Marsha Reid, P.O. Box 39429, Downey, California 90239. (213) 869-5882

The Crafts Fair Guide, P.O. Box 5508, Mill Valley, California 94942. (415) 332-5499

ShoWhat, 3015 W. Pierce, Phoenix, Arizona 85009. (602) 272-8438

Great Arts and Craft Sales Guidebook, Linda Zeitler, P.O. Box 82212, Phoenix, Arizona 85071. (602) 375-0306

Trade Show and Exhibits Schedule, 633 Third Avenue, New York, NY 10017. (212) 973-4890

International Exhibitors Association, 5501 Backlick Street #200, Springfield, Virginia 22151. (703) 941-3725

International Association of Convention Bureaus, P.O. Box 758, Champaign, Illinois 61820. (217) 359-8881

Tradeshow Week Data Book, 12233 West Olympic Blvd., Suite 236, Los Angeles, California 90064 -9956. (213) 826-5696

International Association of Fairs and Expositions, P.O. Box 985, Springfield, Missouri 65801.

Western Exhibitors, Inc., 2181 Greenwich St., San Francisco, California 94123. (415) 346-6666

Trade Show Bureau, P.O. Box 797 8 Beach Rd., East Orleans, MA 02643. (508) 240-0177

Swap Meets West, 295 N. Broadway #147, Santa Maria, CA 93455. (805) 928-2205

The Merchandiser Group's Guide, Sumner Communications, 72 North St., Suite 201, Danbury, CT 06810. (203) 748-2050

CHAPTER 5

EXHIBITING FACTS AND FORMALITIES

Your Exhibit Space

The amount of display space assigned to an exhibitor and its location at the event site vary greatly from show to show. Promoters of large events usually provide a map showing numbered booth spaces from which exhibitors choose an exact location. Space is sold on a first come, first serve basis. Typically, each space measures approximately 10-feet by 10-feet. If necessary, exhibitors can buy an adjacent booth space, remove the center divider, and have a 10-foot by 20-foot selling area. Sometimes show promoters offer a discount on the purchase of more than one space.

Corner spaces are desirable because they provide exposure to customers from two sides. Promoters charge a premium for corner spots, because the additional exposure usually means additional sales. Corner booths can be worth the extra expense, especially if you have popular items to sell.

Exhibitors often disagree about the best booth locations at a show site. Some exhibitors like being near the entrance. Others prefer the areas near the food and entertainment, places where crowds gather. Personally, I avoid booths near the entrance, because many buyers are reluctant to purchase the first things they see. Shoppers usually prefer to view most of the offerings first, before making their purchases. Spots near food or entertainment concessions have drawbacks, too. People gathering there are occupied with eating or watching the entertainment. In addition, the noise level near these areas often is too loud to give a sales presentation properly. It's safest to choose a booth located in the middle of the exhibit arena, whenever possible.

The large craft fairs and trade shows offer booth spaces that come with an eight-foot back drape and three-foot side drapes to separate each exhibitor. Usually a six-foot or eight-foot display table, chair and waste basket are provided as part of the exhibiting package and included as part of the entry fee.

A convention service, contracted by the show promoter, provides the draped booths. A variety of additional display items such as racks, shelves, easels and pegboards can be rented through the convention service. Plants, flowers, carpeting, table covers and other decorator items also are available for rent. Cleaning services and electrical outlets can be obtained for an additional fee.

At small shows and local craft fairs, booth set-up is unpredictable. Where a display is placed depends on how early the exhibitor arrives to set up and how much space the display requires. This casual approach to space planning can be advantageous to the clever weekend entrepreneur. Since boundaries of each exhibit are not very distinct, exhibitors often can spread their products throughout the show. If permitted by the promoter, integrating merchandise into the exhibits of other vendors can be a successful display technique that makes everything look attractive to the shoppers. When a show is held in someone's home or backyard, exhibitors must be ready to adapt to the environment quickly, so products can be displayed to their best advantage. Regardless of where exhibitors wish to place their displays, the promoter always has the final say about location assignments and displaying of merchandise.

The Show Schedule

Typically, craft fairs and trade shows open at 9:00 a.m. and close at 5:00 p.m. Some shows and meets operate during the evening. Most shows are one to four days in length. Thursdays through Sundays are the most popular days of the week for shows. Exhibitors often are required to set up all equipment and displays the day before the show opens. Always arrive early on opening day. Your exhibit should be in place and you should be ready for business at least one hour before the show officially opens. Use this time to look over other exhibits, survey the competition, and decide what you wish to purchase.

Don't underestimate the importance of setting up your display early. Successful exhibitors need time to relax and get into a positive frame of mind before shoppers arrive. Believe me, nothing is more frustrating than arriving late and rushing to set up the display, while hundreds of potential buyers pass by your booth.

Exhibitors are not permitted to break down their exhibits until the show officially closes. Sometimes an exhibitor's contract requires that vendors wait until all customers have left the selling area before dismantling displays. Fines have been levied against exhibitors who disregarded this rule. Follow this simple request if you want to maintain a good business relationship with the promoters.

Staffing Your Exhibit

No one can be as enthusiastic about your merchandise as you can. Therefore, stay with your exhibit and do the selling personally, whenever possible. Many craft fair promoters require the owner/artist to be present at all times. Sales increase when the buyer can ask questions of the artist/crafter concerning their work. Remaining at your booth is essential if you want to meet and greet potential buyers. When you must leave, always place a sign at your exhibit indicating when you will return.

Occasionally you may wish to exhibit at two shows on the same weekend. Without help to staff the second display, you must get permission from the promoter to leave your tagged merchandise unattended. An unattended exhibit will not produce as many sales without an active sales person to assist customers, but it will allow additional exposure for your products and expand selling opportunities for your business. An unattended exhibit is possible only when the show uses a central cashier system.

Work Requirements

Many small, local craft fairs are produced by individuals who also are artists or crafters. These shows provide low-risk opportunities to gain experience, as well as sales and profit. Usually the exhibitors vending in these shows work together to make these events profitable and affordable to all who participate. Since every participant must assist with the organization, marketing and promotion of the event, the fees charged to participate are relatively low.

With this arrangement, exhibitors work an average of three to six hours for the promoters. Exhibitors can volunteer to address envelopes at the mailing party, work the cash register, bag merchandise, monitor the exhibits for cleanliness and security or clean up after closing. These jobs are essential to the success of the fair. Therefore, if you plan to participate, accept your assignment with a smile and help out where you can.

Collecting The Cash

To encourage and simplify purchasing by craft fair shoppers many promoters set up a central cashier. All merchandise is paid for at one location, before the customer exits the show. This eliminates the need for the exhibitor to take money, make change, collect tax, or bag merchandise. These tasks are all done at the central cashier.

Here's how it works. All merchandise for sale is marked with a stringed price tag. The exhibitor's name, address and phone number are marked on one side of the tag and the price of the item is marked on the other side. Sometimes exhibitors are assigned a show number and that number goes on the tag instead of the exhibitor's name. Customers shop from booth to booth, collecting items they want to buy. Then, shoppers pay for all items before they exit at the central, check-out cashier. The price tags are collected and sorted, and exhibitors are paid based on the tags collected.

The central cashier system has several advantages. The most important advantage is the convenience to the customer. Shoppers pay just once for all items purchased, instead of writing checks or paying cash at every booth. Charge card privileges usually are offered, as well. Exhibitors are free to concentrate on selling. Cash registers are used to keep an accurate accounting of all sales and the monies collected are more secure. The primary disadvantage to this system however, is delayed payment to the vendor. Instead of going home with pockets full of cash and checks, exhibitors must wait two to three weeks to receive the rewards of their efforts.

At shows using a central cashier system, always keep accurate records of all merchandise sold. This is important and necessary should errors appear in your pay check. Discrepancies can be reconciled and corrected accurately and quickly if documentation is available.

When exhibitors must act as cashiers, collecting payments from customers, they should be prepared with all the necessary cashiering supplies. A metal cash box or a soft zipper pouch make secure places to store cash, checks and credit card receipts. When not in use, cash containers should be kept hidden from view. Always bring sufficient petty cash in coins and small denominations of currency for making change. I recommend two rolls of all coins, 20, one-dollar bills, 10 5's, five 10's and two 20's. Bring a tax chart, calculator, receipt book, charge card imprinter, charge slips, pens, and bags to complete your sales supplies.

Having a merchant credit card account and being able to accept credit cards for payment can significantly increase your sales. However, if you accept credit card payments, always make sure the card number has been recorded on the charge slip. Sometimes imprinters don't work properly. After all the information is recorded, ask customers to sign the charge slips and write phone numbers below their names. Having a phone number is very helpful when a charge slip comes back from the bank uncollected and the vendor must track down the customer to get paid. Also, verify the card number with the catalog of invalid numbers before completing the sale.

When accepting personal checks, always ask for a bank guarantee card. If a customer can supply a guarantee card, an exhibitor is less apt to get stuck with a bad check. Be sure to write the number and expiration date of the guarantee card on the front of the check, and make sure you have the customer's phone number on the check, too. Years of experience accepting charge cards and checks confirms that most people are honest. When a bad check or invalid charge card is encountered, most exhibitors are promptly paid by the customer after they are called about the problem.

Sharing Space

When you discover a show that appears to offer a fabulous potential for sales, but you can't afford the exhibitor's fee, consider sharing space with another vendor. With careful planning, a 10-foot by 10-foot booth can provide enough space for two weekend entrepreneurs to adequately sell their goods.

When possible, share space with an exhibitor you know and would enjoy working with on show day. Select exhibitors whose products complement your merchandise and are not in direct competition. For example, I sell personalized children's books. I have shared space successfully with vendors offering children's items such as clothing, wooden toys, and hair bows. When selecting a partner to share booth space, give highest priority to vendors whose products also appeal to your customer base.

Exhibitors who share space can display merchandise in two ways, either by integrating products or by separating them. When integrating merchandise, the goal is to arrange the items together to project one cohesive image, one coordinated display. For example, if one vendor sells sterling silver jewelry and the other sells hand-dyed silk scarves and blouses, the jewelry items should be displayed as accessories for the clothing. The vendors can attach silver pins to the scarves or display a necklace with each blouse. A well coordinated exhibit makes use of both exhibitor's items, integrating them throughout the entire display. By combining all the merchandise the display becomes more attractive. This cohesive look can enhance the attractiveness of both exhibitors' products and produce more sales.

The second option is to keep all merchandise separate. This method works best when one exhibitor has products that appeal to the show's general audience, but not to the other vendor's specific customers. The key to success in this situation is to separate the merchandise, as much as possible, so the display looks like two distinctly separate businesses.

Sharing space not only saves money, it also offers other advantages. The companionship of another exhibitor helps maintain motivation, doubles the sales force and gives each exhibitor a chance to rest for a minute away from the booth when it's time to grab lunch or use the restroom facilities.

While sharing space offers many advantages, always check with the promoter in advance to see if booth sharing is permitted. Some shows have restrictions on how many vendors can occupy one booth, or how many different company signs will be permitted to identify a space. Insurance and licensing requirements also differ from show to show and may restrict sharing. Always get permission to share space before you sign an exhibitor's contract. This will prevent any embarrassment or difficulties the day of the event.

Exhibit Security

When participating in a craft fair or trade show that runs for several days, overnight security becomes a concern. At indoor events, most promoters will hire security personnel to guard the exhibits after everyone leaves. If this is the case, keep all expensive merchandise hidden from view or take it with you and return it the next day. Many exhibitors cover their merchandise and displays with bed sheets or cloth covers to discourage theft.

When a show is held outdoors, or when no security is provided overnight, exhibitors must decide which items can remain at the site and which need to be removed for safe keeping. It is tiring to set up and take down an entire display three days in a row. Nevertheless, sometimes it is necessary in order to secure the merchandise.

Set Goals For Every Show

Each event requires time and money in preparation. In addition, two or three days may be spent working at the show. Therefore, successful weekend entrepreneurs must attempt to get the maximum return for their investment of time and money.

To assure success of your weekend business, set concrete goals to accomplish at every show. Goal setting directs your efforts and gives purpose to your actions. When exhibitors have several goals to achieve, they have more chances to succeed. The primary reason for exhibiting is to sell products and make money. Other worthwhile goals include:

1. Building a mailing list of potential customers.

2. Introducing a new product and assessing consumer reaction.

3. Gathering market information by talking to shoppers and identifying needs and wants.

4. Obtaining new sales leads.

5. Meeting suppliers, distributors, and other vendors that can help build your business.

6. Recruiting sales personnel.

7. Building public recognition for your company and product line.

8. Educating the buying public about your products.

9. Gaining exposure for your business, while improving your sales skills.

Always make a list of goals to accomplish at every event you schedule. The sample list that follows demonstrates how to set very specific goals.

SHOW GOALS

SHOW: **DATE:**

ACTUAL FIGURES

Today, I will sell $_____worth of products. $_____

I will hand out _____brochures to qualified prospects. _____

I will obtain _____qualified customer leads.   _____

I will give _____product demonstrations.   _____

I will meet _____new distributors.   _____

I will find out about _____new shows.   _____

I will give _____sales presentations.   _____

I will discover _____new ideas.   _____

Exhibitor Etiquette

Yes, there are general rules of etiquette that govern the actions of exhibitors, and it's wise to practice them. Experienced vendors on the trade show circuit are aware of these rules, but many crafters and new exhibitors are not familiar with them. The common sense rules listed below will keep the customers and other exhibitors happy and will contribute to making your experience pleasant and successful, too.

Don't Smoke

Many convention centers prohibit smoking at the displays. Even when it is permitted, don't do it. Smoking at your booth will anger the adjacent exhibitors who do not smoke, and will alienate customers, as well. If you must smoke, go to the designated smoking area away from the show site.

Don't Tie Up Exhibitors With Idle Conversation

Sharing ideas and making friends with other exhibitors is part of the fun associated with exhibit marketing. Just remember though, other vendors have paid money to exhibit and sell their products, and that is their first priority. Exhibitors cannot acknowledge and qualify prospects if they are engaged in a discussion with another exhibitor. Customers often are reluctant to interrupt with questions when an exhibitor is talking to someone. Be alert during conversations with vendors and always excuse yourself when a prospect approaches. If things are slow in your booth, don't bother other exhibitors when they are busy with customers.

Don't Develop A Negative Attitude

Nothing is more annoying than a neighboring exhibitor who moans, groans and complains about the show. Exhibitors have blamed everything from the promoter, the advertising, the customers, the location and the weather for bad results. Some will try to occupy other exhibitors' time complaining. Negative talk is unproductive and self defeating. Even when sales are poor, it is useless to dwell on it. Rather than grumble about a slow show, use the time to make notes on possible reasons why attendance was poor, or why your products did not sell. Rearrange your merchandise, go over your sales presentation, make sure your deodorant is working. No matter how unhappy you are, keep your complaints to yourself.

Don't Eat In View Of The Customers

Leave your booth when you wish to eat. If you are working a show by yourself, it may be impossible to get away for a lunch break. If you must eat at your booth, do so as inconspicuously as possible.

Don't "Badmouth" The Competition

My mother told me many times, "If you don't have something nice to say, don't say anything." Every exhibitor should heed those words. Believe it or not, some exhibitors think the only way they can make a sale is to verbally rundown their competition. For example, I heard a T-shirt vendor discourage customers from purchasing from a competitor by telling them the competitor uses inferior materials. One of my customers reported to me that a competitor said my products would fall apart. This type of behavior is improper and unprofessional.

Today's consumers are sophisticated. They rarely are swayed by negative comments, and often resent the vendor who makes them. Never "badmouth" the competition in an attempt to make your items look better. You'll do best if you sell your products on their own merits.

Don't Leave Your Booth Unoccupied For Long Periods

Sometimes it is necessary to leave your booth unattended, especially when you are working the show alone. Try to avoid leaving the display area for extended periods. If you must leave, place a sign for everyone to see indicating when you will be back. That way, if customers need to see you, they will know when to return to your exhibit.

Don't Make Excessive Noise

This problem usually occurs when an exhibitor has a piece of equipment or a product that is noisy. Most shows have restrictions on products or display props that produce excessive noise. Sometimes disturbing noise is the result of carelessness and poor planning on the part of the offending party.

When the volume is too high on video equipment used in a presentation or a tape recorder used to demonstrate a musical tape, other vendors in the area will not be able to converse with customers. Offensive noise also can come from salespeople who talk too loud. Make sure the sound of your sales presentation stays within the confines of your space.

Don't Bring Children Or Pets

This may seem obvious, but I still find shows where children of exhibitors run in and out of each booth, handling merchandise and making a general nuisance of themselves. A mother who brings an infant to a small, local show may be able to manage, without too much difficulty. But, when young children run wild throughout the exhibits, it's disturbing and inappropriate.

Pets also do not belong at your exhibit. Pets are miserable at hot, outdoor shows where they may not receive enough water or attention, and dog "do-do" on the grass next to a booth is disgusting. Most large, high-profile trade shows and craft fairs restrict children and pets. Unfortunately, many small craft events have no rules on the subjects. Hire a babysitter and leave pets at home. Then, you won't alienate other exhibitors and will be invited back by the promoter.

Don't Enter Other Exhibits Without The Owner's Permission

This rule is strictly enforced on the trade show circuit. You must ask permission to enter any exhibit space that is not your own. If permission to enter is granted, be ready to excuse yourself if a potential customer enters.

Don't Extend Your Sales Efforts Outside Your Space

This rule pertains to display fixtures, as well as sales personnel, and is strictly enforced at trade shows. Chairs, racks, signs or other items are not permitted to extend into the aisles or beyond the assigned boundaries. Personnel staffing a booth may not solicit customers from outside the exhibit area, unless specific arrangements have been made with the promoter. For example, a promoter might permit a costumed character to circulate among customers at the event, giving away discount coupons printed with the booth number of an exhibitor.

CHAPTER 6

APPLYING TO FAIRS, SHOWS & MEETS

Entry Fees

Entry fees for craft fairs and trade shows vary greatly. Large, well-established shows charge entry fees in the range of $200 to $1,500 for one space. Large shows offering strong advertising plans and ideal locations for your customer base, may be worth the expense to exhibit, since they often can draw 10,000 to 20,000 potential buyers. Large shows often generate large profits. Even so, the beginner should gain experience exhibiting and selling at smaller shows before attempting the larger, more expensive ones.

Entrepreneurs with little or no experience at exhibit marketing should practice their skills first, at local events that charge low entry fees. These events are held at schools, churches, and private residences. The average fee for exhibit space ranges from $20 to $100. Some promoters also take an additional 10 to 15 percent commission on the vendor's total sales. The best, local craft fairs can draw several thousand people during a weekend. They provide ample opportunity for sales and profit, as well as the chance to develop sales and presentation skills. The average fee for rental space at swap meets ranges from $10 to $20.

Book Events Early

Smart weekend entrepreneurs take their businesses seriously. They keep track of operating expenses and budget the necessary capital to invest in the best show opportunities available. Most trade show and craft fair promoters book exhibitors three to six months in advance of the actual show date. To be considered as a possible vendor, the show application and entry fee must be sent to promoters promptly. This means vendors must commit a substantial amount of cash in July and August, for example, to pay for the high-profile, holiday shows occurring in October through December. Plan carefully so the cash outlay will not be a financial hardship and you have the funds available to apply to shows held during the biggest, money-making season.

Jury Procedures

Many craft fairs require first-time applicants to submit their products to a jury for evaluation before they can be accepted. This process is like an audition. To be considered, vendors must submit slides or photos of their work and their display along with their application. The promoter assembles a jury, or a judging committee, to review each application and decide which applicants will be admitted to the show. Some promoters ask exhibitors to meet and interview personally with the committee.

The prestigious arts and crafts fairs are very competitive. Since they have far more applicants than space available, they maintain strict entry requirements and have long waiting lists. Many shows limit the number of competing products, and acceptance one year does not automatically guarantee acceptance to the show in future years.

Whenever a group of people make decisions regarding the acceptance of an applicant, politics and human nature will enter into the process. Therefore, use every possible angle to increase your chances for acceptance, if you have a strong desire to exhibit in a specific show.

Always apply early. The date your application is received by the promoter could make a difference. For example, if two applicants make pottery and the jury must decide between two equally talented potters, the postmark on the application may be the tie-breaking factor.

Always read the application thoroughly before completing it. Follow the directions carefully and complete the application accurately the first time. If possible, type the application or at least print legibly. Include on the application any special requests you have, like electricity or extra storage space.

Unless instructed not to, return the completed application with the full entry fee. Send the full fee even when only a small deposit is required. Money talks, so making an early commitment in dollars might prove helpful in the selection process.

If promoters require photos or slides with the application, it's a clear indication they are looking for exhibitors who take a professional approach to their business. Hire a professional photographer to take both photos and slides of your products and your display. Spend the time and money necessary to make your presentation excellent--one that best reflects the quality of your items and your ability to display and merchandise them.

The jury will be using the photos or slides to look at the materials and workmanship of the products closely. Include examples of your inexpensive items, as well as the expensive ones. Take close-up shots of the merchandise, photographing your finest quality work. When photographing your exhibit, never include people in the picture. Select the best shots and make several copies of each.

Most applications request 5 to 10 different slides or photos of your work. Duplicate photo sets are necessary if you apply to several shows scheduled close together. With only one set of photos, you may not receive it back from one promoter in time to send it to another.

When slides are requested, mail them in clear plastic slide holders. This will allow the committee to pass around the slides without worrying about damaging them with fingerprints. Slide holders can be found at any camera shop.

All slides must be labeled. Include your name, phone number, a description of the item, including its dimensions and completion date, on each slide frame. Type the information on adhesive-backed, white mailing labels. Cut the typed labels carefully and place them on each slide frame. Then, slip the slides into the holder. Include a self-addressed, stamped envelope and a note asking the jury to return the slides.

Getting Accepted

Emphasize your uniqueness when filling out the application. Determine what distinguishes your merchandise from that of hundreds of other applicants seeking acceptance. First, ask the following questions. Have you exhibited in this particular show before? Have you added some new products to your line? Do you know someone in the sponsoring organization? Did someone with influence suggest you apply? Have you received some favorable publicity in the local newspapers or on local TV? Include supporting information in a note attached to your application. Send along copies of any publicity, too.

Another way to gain attention is to include information about your promotional abilities in the comments section of the application. Be sure to mention if you hold a demonstration at your exhibit, or if your product is one that attracts people and involves them in hands-on activity. For example, one exhibitor wrote, "We encourage everyone to handle our music boxes and wind chimes. For this reason, people enjoy gathering at our booth. If accepted, please put us at a location that can accommodate a crowd."

The promoter or jury must choose exhibitors based on the information contained in each application and shown in slides and photos. Therefore, make sure your application stands out and communicates your professionalism. Sell your abilities and expertise as a weekend entrepreneur. Present your product's strong points and communicate to the jury that your display will be an asset to the show.

If Rejected, Don't Give Up

If you are turned down for an important show, don't give up. A few steps still remain that could get you accepted. These steps work for both craft fairs and trade shows.

After receiving a rejection letter, call the promoter every two weeks to inquire about exhibitor cancellations. Tell the promoter you are interested in any space that might become available, and leave your name and telephone number. Don't expect a call back, just make sure the promoter remembers your name. In the meantime, continue to call regularly. If a cancellation occurs, you may be able to fill the space.

Next, ask if any of the accepted exhibitors requested permission to share space. Some shows will go out of their way to match exhibitors wishing to share a booth. They want to fill as many spaces as possible with enthusiastic vendors.

As a last resort, one approach can be tried that might secure a display space and could get you a substantial discount off the entry fee. This approach is risky and there's no guarantee that it will work every time. Load your vehicle with your display and merchandise and arrive at the show at least an hour before starting time. Go to the check-in desk, and ask if there are any spaces that didn't sell or if anyone canceled at the last minute. Unsold space and cancellations are always possible, especially at trade shows. If space is available, say you will take it if they will offer a discount on the exhibit fee. Again, this approach is risky, but when it works an exhibitor often gets a great spot at half the normal fee. If you are lucky enough to succeed in getting a space, keep your good fortune to yourself. Otherwise, you may never get another chance to exhibit at that show again. It's understandable that promoters do not wish to publicize the fact that some exhibitors paid less for their space.

Guidelines For Getting Accepted Into The Best Shows

Apply early.

Type or print the application neatly.

Send professional slides and photos of your products and display.

Include the full entry fee with the application.

Include a note about the uniqueness and desirability of your products and display.

Mention influential people.

If rejected, try alternate methods.

Be persistent, but pleasant.

CHAPTER 7

CREATING A DYNAMIC DISPLAY

Stop and Look!! That's what effective displays must say to shoppers passing by. Exhibitors must fight for attention, so the most attractive, unusual or eye-catching displays are the ones that get noticed. With that in mind, don't take the construction of your exhibit and the merchandising of your products for granted.

Merchandising is everything you do to attract shoppers and get them to buy your products. So, pay careful attention to such details as the accent colors of the display, the methods employed to present products, the materials utilized to construct the display and the signs that identify your business.

The entire selling environment should reflect the right image and attract customers most likely to purchase your offerings. The first step necessary to create an effective display is to design the type of structure that will best present your products or services. Then, select the materials to construct it.

There are many designs to consider when planning your display and exhibit layout. The simplest way to determine which type is best for you is to study the displays of local crafters, trade show exhibitors and retail merchants. Your display will establish your image and either enhance or detract from the appeal of your products. Therefore, take special care in planning and creating it.

When planning a display, determine how your products are best viewed by the buyer? Should they be displayed at eye level, suspended from above, placed on shelves, hung on a wall, or laid on the floor? Next, consider your exhibit theme, if any, and what props will enhance the presentation of your goods or services. Then, give some thought to the ease of assembly, time required for set-up and break-down, weight of the materials and transportation requirements of your exhibit.

Many weekend entrepreneurs just starting their businesses have limited funds with which to develop a display. Lots of creativity, imagination and resourcefulness, however, can make up for lack of money. This chapter will provide many ideas for low-cost construction materials and items you can use to create an attractive and effective display to showcase your merchandise or services.

Basic Display Structures

Tables

The most commonly used display structure is the lightweight, folding table. Aluminum tables are inexpensive and can be found at most do-it-yourself building supply stores. Tables are available in five, six or eight foot lengths, and usually are two or two-and-a-half feet wide. Six-foot tables are the most popular, since they allow for a wide variety of configurations.

Table Configurations

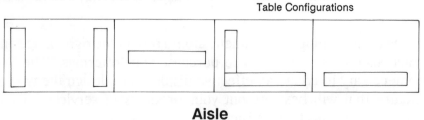

Aisle

Table Configurations

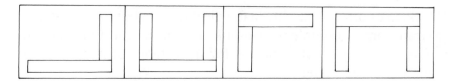

Aisle

Tables also can be made by simply laying a piece of plywood, in any desired size, over two saw horses. When draped with a cloth, these make-shift tables look fine. Tables also can be made by cutting a hollow door in half, hinging it back together and laying it over metal legs.

Shelves

Shelves offer versatility in the display area, but they must be easy to transport and simple to assemble to be practical. One of the most popular ways to make shelves for a portable display is to use a wooden, three-panel screen as a base and use 1-foot by 6-foot plywood boards as shelves. Another shelf display can be made by attractively painting two, six-foot step ladders and placing plywood boards or wooden dowels across each rung of the ladder.

Panels

Panels form the basis of many interesting and effective displays. Many are lightweight and easy for one person to handle. Panels are versatile and can be used in a variety of configurations. In addition, many low-cost materials such as pegboard, lattice, metal grids and grooved wallboard can be used to construct display panels.

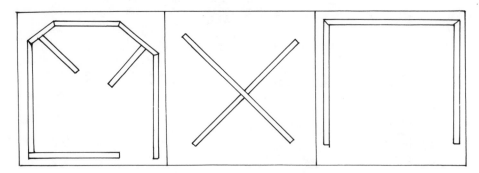

Aisle

Pegboard

Framed artwork, calligraphy or photography needs a backdrop to be effectively displayed. Pegboard is an excellent display material, since it is very versatile and inexpensive. An "X" frame or "A" frame display can be fashioned from pegboard. These display styles are easy to erect and transport. Another option is to construct a triangular display of pegboard. This style allows three sides for displaying products.

By placing hooks or piping around the perimeter of an exhibit area, 4-foot by 6-foot sheets of pegboard can be hung to provide a flat display surface. Another alternative is to mount sheets of pegboard on wooden or metal legs. A variety of metal hooks, plexiglass display pieces and shelf fixtures are made specifically for use with pegboard. You can find these items at outlets that sell store display fixtures. Look in the Yellow Pages under "Display."

Lattice

An inexpensive, but attractive material to use in a display is wooden lattice. Found at most building supply stores, lattice usually is available in 4-foot by 8-foot sheets. Don't buy flimsy lattice used for garden plants and flowers. Use lattice with thick diagonal slats.

This material is excellent for displaying items that should be hung, such as clothing or dried flower arrangements. Hang lattice in the same manner as pegboard, from piping around the perimeter of the booth. Lattice panels also can be mounted on legs or made into folding screens.

Wire Grid Panels

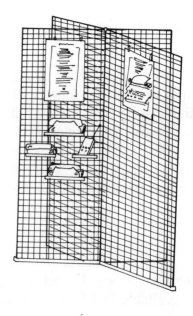

Wire grid panels can be assembled in a variety of ways, and can easily be expanded to fit your changing needs. Many accessories and display attachments such as baskets, shelves, hooks, railings and trays can be purchased for use with wire grids. Wire grids can create a very professional, attractive and durable display. They are, however, expensive and very heavy to transport and erect.

Modular Wire Cubes

Modular wire cubes are popular and are an inexpensive alternative to heavy, metal wire grids. Small and easy to assemble, the cubes are made of lightweight, plastic-coated wire panels that snap together with plastic connectors. Assemble an entire wall of cubes or a small custom unit to display shirts, gift items, sporting goods or any stackable merchandise. Mini grids come in several colors and utilize the same accessories as heavy wire grids.

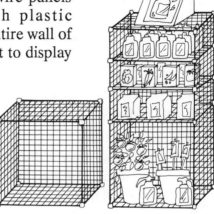

Slatwall Panels

Slatwall panels, also known as grooved wallboard, is a multi-purpose display material. Although heavy, grooved slatboard comes in 4-foot by 8-foot sheets which can be cut to any size. The grooves separating each slat of wood are designed to hold display fixtures such as hooks, baskets, and shelves. The panels come ready to paint, laminated in colored finishes, or finished in a variety of wood veneers.

Professional Exhibiting Units

Several companies design and manufacture exhibits specifically for use at trade shows. These high-tech, portable units offer many modular designs. Some use velcro background surfaces to display photos, graphs, or printed information. Some incorporate giant photomurals that grab customer's attention. Others offer counters and pedestals to showcase products. Professional displays are expensive. Nevertheless, they will be an excellent investment if your primary selling arena will be trade shows, since your display actually becomes your traveling store. If you need a professionally manufactured exhibit unit for a specific trade show, but are not able to purchase one, some companies will rent them on a per show basis.

In addition, many display companies have manufacturing capabilities and can customize a display to your exact specifications. They can build anything, from a simple backdrop to a vendor cart similar to those seen in shopping malls. You may wish to consider these options, after you have some experience and are ready to upgrade your display.

Tents And Awnings

Vendors who regularly exhibit outside should consider investing in a portable tent or awning. Tents and awnings come in many  configurations and materials. Most use an aluminum or PVC pipe frame, with a canvas or vinyl covering that fits over the assembly. Vendors that make and sell them for a reasonable fee usually can be found at flea markets or swap meets. Awning companies also stock a variety of tents and awnings suitable for exhibitors and will rent them, as well.

Professional Signs

Signs that identify your business or communicate sales messages to shoppers are an important part of an exhibitor's display. Many sign companies are able to produce colorful, professionally lettered signs or banners the same day you order them. Give careful thought to the colors, style of the lettering and size of your company sign and coordinate these elements with those on your sales literature whenever possible. A logo or company symbol on your sign helps to reinforce your identity to the public.

The size of the sign and the lettering will determine how easy it is to read. Keep in mind three-inch lettering can be read from 70 to 80 feet and one-inch lettering from 10 to 30 feet. Avoid hand lettering any signs yourself, unless you are a graphic artist. Hire a sign company and give your booth a professional image with professional looking signs. Remember, a business with no sign, is a sign of no business.

Product Presentation

Elevate Your Products

Selecting a design and deciding on the basic construction materials is just the first step to creating an appealing environment from which to sell your goods and services. The next step involves a bit of showmanship and imagination, since the presentation of products and the props used to complement your display have a big impact on catching the shopper's attention and drawing the customer to your booth.

It should be obvious that just laying products flat on a table or piling them on shelves isn't the best way to display them. Yet, many vendors do just that, then wonder why things aren't selling. One of the most important principles of good product presentation is elevation. Dimension and depth can be added to your display and products can be placed closer to eye level by elevating them in a variety of ways.

Any number of methods can be used to add height to your products and give your display extra impact. An assortment of cardboard boxes, plastic containers, upside-down flower pots, crates, bricks, tiles or wooden boards can provide a variety of different levels on which to place your products.

Vendors with rustic items, can use crates or bricks in their natural state to elevate and display their items and enhance the theme of their display. Fabric draped over boxes or brightly painted containers are effective props that elevate merchandise. Vendors selling portable phone systems or some other sophisticated merchandise, might use plexiglass risers or mirrored cubes to display their goods. Just use your imagination and plan out a display theme consistent with your merchandise and the expectations of your customer.

Use Props

Every exhibitor should go to the nearest shopping mall and spend an afternoon looking at the display windows and making notes on how props are used by window designers. Props can create a theme, add impact, demonstrate usage, and provide functional assistance in presenting products to their best advantage. When props are used to help create a theme, they provide continuity and allow products to be displayed in a cohesive, well-blended manner.

For example, an exhibitor who sells hand-woven, wool sweaters and shawls might place an authentic weaver's loom in the middle of the booth as the focal point. Sweaters can be displayed from the drawers of an antique pine dresser, on an antique dressmaker's dummy or stacked in an old, open trunk.

Likewise, a vendor selling dolls could use baby doll furniture as props. Displaying a doll in a rocking chair, high chair or cradle would add an appealing touch to the display and capture the shopper's interest.

Containers also make great props. They can be integrated throughout a display and filled with selected merchandise. Baskets, barrels, crates, flower pots, fish bowls, mugs, trunks and brass pots are just a few containers that have been successfully incorporated into displays. Colorful tissue placed in containers also produces a dramatic effect.

For props to have impact, they must be creative, even outrageous! Vendors who sell jewelry or sunglasses, for example, might consider covering a display table with sand and beach towels and have items draped over interesting pieces of driftwood or coming out of beautiful sea shells.

A terrific display was developed by a woman who sells recharged laser printer cartridges at a considerable discount off the price of new ones. Because the product itself does not make an attractive or interesting display piece, the vendor had to think of some way to catch the attention of people passing by her booth. Her booth design was extremely creative, effective and low-cost. From a solid color backdrop, she fashioned a waterfall of oversized $100 bills cascading into a trash can. Her booth sign read "WHY THROW YOUR MONEY AWAY." Since her customers are business owners interested in cutting expenses, her booth design attracted immediate attention and provided an opening for her to explain how recharged cartridges could save money.

Another way to gain attention is to display a product in use. Show customers what they can do with the product after they make the purchase. For example, create a breeze from a fan to demonstrate the sounds of windchimes. Stained glass ornaments can be displayed by hanging them from a lighted Christmas tree, a window pane or a fireplace mantel. Hand-woven baskets can be filled with fruit, letters, condiments and bath products. A hand-blown vase can be filled with flowers, potpourri, or colored marbles. Painted silk scarfs can be tied around a hat or displayed as a belt.

Props that provide functional assistance can help facilitate the sale of products. Vendors who sell clothing should have a full-length mirror and a dressing area available, so customers can try on the items. A hand-held mirror to view jewelry and earrings, a stool to sit on while trying on shoes, a tapeplayer to hear seminar tapes, or tissues to wipe off makeup samples are examples of functional props necessary to provide assistance to the customer and help sell products. Some props are decorative and some are functional. Take time to consider which type would enhance your display and improve your selling opportunities.

Offer Samples

Customers flock to booths that give free samples. Sampling, as a method to entice sales, has worked successfully for vendors with products such as cookies, cinnamon rolls, salsa, pickles, coffee, tea, make-up, perfumes, flowers or stationery. If you decide to use this method to attract customers, be sure to consider whether the benefits of sampling outweigh the costs. Always provide printed material and ordering information with each sample.

Theme Merchandise And Holiday Packaging

Profits can be increased tremendously if vendors develop product lines that revolve around the themes of holidays and special events. Whenever possible, make or stock special items that tie into a specific holiday season. If this is not possible, consider packaging what you offer in a creative way that reflects the holiday or decorating your display in the holiday theme. For example, give a carnation with each purchase on Valentine's Day and a chocolate rose on Mother's Day. Gift wrap your products in holiday papers. Add

sparklers to the package for the Fourth of July or a green clover for St. Patrick's Day. Decorating themes for displays also can come from current events. Remember how effectively American flags and yellow ribbons were used to lure customers during the Persian Gulf War. Special items and theme packaging attract customers and encourage them to buy. Below is a list of some of the occasions and holiday themes to plan for as part of your merchandising effort.

Valentine's Day	St. Patrick's Day
Easter	Tax Season
Mother's Day	Father's Day
July Fourth	Back to School
Halloween	Thanksgiving
Hanukkah	Christmas
New Years	President's Day
Labor Day	New Baby
Marriages	Graduation
Communion	Birthdays
Anniversarys	Elections

Table Coverings

Most trade shows and some craft fairs will provide draping for your table as part of the entry fee. For those that don't, you should acquire a custom table covering that will complement your products and display. All sides of your tables that are exposed to the public should be covered to within a few inches from the floor. The easiest way to cover a table is to drape it with a rectangular piece of cloth that covers all sides. Always gather the excess cloth at the corners and pin it back, so no one will trip over the cover. Placing another cloth of a contrasting color or a deeper hue over the top of the table can make the display more attractive.

As your business grows, invest some of your profits to improve your display. While a pinned-back cloth is cheap and easy, the serious weekend entrepreneur eventually will invest in a more sophisticated table covering. For example, I hired an interior design firm to custom make a table covering in specific colors with my company name and logo appliqued on the front. The table cover was designed to snugly fit over a 6-foot table. The unique covering has become a  very identifiable part of my display. My customers easily recognize it when searching for my booth at a large show.

Want to put more pizzazz in your table display? Find ways to incorporate some unusual materials into the presentation of your products. Vendors have created attractive table covers using quilts, grass cloth, straw mats, cork board and beach towels. Others have used marbles, tissue paper, cotton balls, rhinestones, sand and confetti to create interest and accent their products.

Use Color Consistently

Businesses using specific colors and distinguishing logos to identify the company should use the same colors and logo in the design of their displays. Consistent use of color is an effective way to gain name recognition and company identification, especially for companies who frequently utilize exhibit marketing.

When choosing color to accent your display and table coverings, pick colors that contrast with your products. Blue, black and red are good choices, but always select colors that will enhance the products. Avoid fabrics with busy patterns. Solid colors never detract from the product. Children's items are displayed best with pastels or bright primary colors. Jewelry and sculpture sell better when displayed against a black background. Black, navy and gray are colors that are more sophisticated and give a business-like impression.

Fire Regulations

Most shows require exhibitors to comply with strict fire safety rules and regulations established by local authorities. Be safe and make sure all display materials are fire retardant. The district Fire Marshal often does on-site, random flame tests at most shows. This means the Marshal may come to your booth and place a lighted match to the bottom of your table covering to see if it will burn.

If you employ a professional design company to make your table covering, ask the designer to use flame retardant materials. You also can apply a variety of spray-on or wash-in flame retardant products to your exhibit materials or hire a company to do it for you. Look in the Yellow Pages under "flameproofing" for companies specializing in this service and at the hardware stores for the self-application products. Consult the Fire Marshal in your area for complete information regarding fire safety rules and regulations.

Lighting

Most retailers believe that lighting affects sales; more light equals more sales. The question is, how many more sales will be produced for the cost of additional lighting? At most shows, electrical connections available at the booth space will cost an additional $35 to $50, and lighting fixtures can cost several hundred dollars.

Determine if lighting is essential to your product presentation. Vendors selling fine art or intricate items with lots of detail, find they need spotlights to illuminate the work and help customers appreciate the quality of the craftsmanship.

Some vendors exhibiting indoors with low light, supplement the overhead lighting to increase the illumination of the entire booth space. Most indoor shows, however, are held in large exhibit halls with excellent lighting. In addition, shows held outdoors during the day usually require no additional lighting.

Most promoters limit a vendor's power allotment to 500 watts. Eight, 60-watt bulbs will provide adequate lighting for a 10-foot by 10-foot booth. For spotlighting, the clip-on fixtures with concave, aluminum reflector shells work best. These can be clipped onto frames, shelves, tables or overhead piping. Carefully consider what lighting is important for your display needs, before you invest in any fixtures. If your electrical needs are extensive, you may wish to buy a portable generator, as well.

If lighting is essential, purchase the best quality fixtures you can afford. Durable, well-made equipment that can withstand time and travel is a wise investment. Include a 100-foot, heavy-duty extension cord, a six-outlet electric strip and a three-prong adapter with your electrical supplies.

Getting Organized

The smart weekend entrepreneur knows the advantages of preparing for each exhibiting event several days in advance. Careful attention to details prevents costly mistakes, like forgetting the cash box, neglecting to pack advertising literature or leaving behind the tools necessary to erect your display. Checklists of your inventory and supplies will insure against such disasters.

Start by making a complete list of all the products you will sell at each exhibiting event. Create a list that catagorizes each item by color, size, style or other descriptive characteristics that can help you track inventory after each show. Use this list as a sales record. Not only will it help you with restocking and reordering merchandise, it will make it easy to evaluate which items did or did not sell at each event.

Separate all the items you will bring to each event into categories such as display materials, sales literature, cashiering supplies, tools, personal necessities and product inventory. Make a checklist of every item in each category down to the last paper clip, then make copies of each. Plastic tubs and heavy cardboard boxes are excellent containers for storing and transporting your merchandise and supplies. Place the list of contents on the outside of each container. Check off items as you fill each container with one category of supplies. The items will vary from business to business, but some common essentials are listed below.

Personal Necessities

Drinking water	Cups
Sun tan lotion	Sunglasses
Wash cloth	Soap
Tissues	Hat or Visor
Mirror	Comb or Brush
Chapstick	Aspirin
Cough drops	Bandaids
Tweezers	

Cashiering Supplies

Pens	Pencils
Calculator	Tax chart
Receipt book	Bags
Charge card imprinter	Charge card sales slips
Petty cash	Price tags
Scotch tape	

Tool Box

Scissors	Duct tape
Hammer	Nails
Screw driver	Screws
Wrench	Plyers
Staple gun	Staples
Tacks	Glue
Magic markers	Pen knife
Wire cutters	Wire
Heavy rope	Flashlight
Fire extinguisher	String

Purchase a heavy-duty hand truck or cart for transporting your display and supplies from your vehicle to the show site. Sometimes the walk is quite long, so the fewer trips the better.

Include several large sheets of heavy, clear plastic in your supplies. The type of plastic sheets found at paint and hardware stores, commonly used as painter's drop cloths, work well. If it rains while you are working an outdoor show, the clear plastic sheets will protect the merchandise from getting wet and still allow customers to see what is offered.

Bring your own food. The food sold at most craft fairs, trade shows and swap meets is usually overpriced and unhealthy. Since most exhibitors work at least eight hours, pack some healthy meals and plenty of fruit and snacks to sustain your energy.

Load your vehicle the evening before the show to eliminate the possibility of forgetting something in the morning rush to get on the road. Plan enough time to have coffee or to eat breakfast before you leave the house, so you can relax and get into a positive frame of mind on your way to the event.

Be A Prepared Exhibitor

Inventory your supplies and mark off each item on the checklist attached to each supply container to guard against forgetting essentials. Then, pack your merchandise and supplies in the easy-to-carry containers and load your vehicle the evening before the event.

Summary

For a display to stand out from hundreds of others, it must have impact. Impact is achieved by carefully planning the details of the exhibit and incorporating the following:

* A theme to attract attention.
* Color identification for easy recognition.
* Methods to elevate your products.

* Props to enhance product presentation.
* Professional signs to identify the vendor.
* Adequate lighting to illuminate the merchandise.

For a display to be practical for exhibit marketing, it also must be:

* Able to fit into your vehicle.
* Easy to transport from your vehicle to your display area.
* Lightweight.
* Simple to assemble.
* Quick to break-down.
* Durable to withstand repeat use.

CHAPTER 8

SHARPEN YOUR SALES SKILLS

Don't Skip This Chapter!

Whether you sell crafts or computers, developing an effective sales presentation is fundamental to your success as a weekend entrepreneur. Sales experts maintain that vendors must grab the attention of a shopper in 3.5 seconds. So, a well-conceived plan of attack is absolutely essential. Displays should be designed to attract shoppers. But even with an exceptional display, sales will not occur if the vendor is unable to communicate product information that is informative, professional and persuasive, once the customer enters the booth.

A weekend entrepreneur's business revolves around selling. Money is made only when something is sold. Therefore, exhibitors must become comfortable with the selling process in order to succeed. Unfortunately, many artists, crafters, and manufacturers love to create and produce their products, but hate to sell them. Much of the dislike for selling is derived from the notion that good salespeople must be aggressive and pushy. With some preparation and practice, anyone can improve their selling skills and become comfortable making sales presentations, without changing character or resorting to high-pressure selling tactics.

Projecting A Professional Image

Never underestimate the impact your personality and appearance have on your selling abilities and your profits. Getting one chance to make a first impression applies to every exhibitor. The overall image you and your display project will determine whether a shopper will stop at your booth or pass by it. Selling yourself, by using methods that influence the customer's perception of you, can contribute to a shopper's willingness to buy from you.

Clothes That Make The Sale

The typical artist or crafter thinks mostly of comfort when dressing for a show. This is evidenced by the casual, and sometimes sloppy, appearance of their attire and grooming. Trade show exhibitors, on the other hand, are apt to dress more conservatively, in business attire, especially if the show is attracting other business men and women. A quick examination of the exhibitors at any craft fair or trade show proves the point that some make a better impression than others. Those that project the most appealing image have dressed to complement their display, dressed in the clothing they sell, or dressed in the style of the shoppers attending.

An exhibitor who dresses to complement a display, wears clothing that enhances the appeal of the products or emphasizes the theme of the exhibit. For example, the female vendor selling country crafts could wear a vintage dress, bonnet and shawl. A vendor selling baked goods might wear a decorative apron with a baker's hat. Someone selling medical or health supplies may choose to wear a lab coat. A vendor representing a South Pacific cruise line could wear Hawaiian garb, complete with a fresh flower lei.

Exhibitors that use imagination in selecting what they will wear at a show can give their display the extra impact that could provide a competitive edge. With little effort, the people staffing a booth can be an added attraction to the display.

If it is possible to wear what you sell, by all means do it. Earrings, jewelry, clothing, shoes, belts, hats and scarves are just a few of the items vendors can model. Occasionally taking a walk among the shoppers at the show to model your outfit or accessories is a great way to create interest in your products. Carry a small sign indicating your company name and booth number. Pass out your business cards with your booth number on the back to interested prospects. A friend of mine creates a rush of customers to her booth by having her husband and daughter walk through the show dressed in matching, hand-painted clothing she makes.

By using information gathered from show promoters and other vendors, an exhibitor should be able to determine a show's atmosphere in advance. The show's location also is a good indication of the type of people likely to attend. Every event has a distinctly different atmosphere. It can be conservative and businesslike, fashionable and sophisticated or casual and sporty. How you dress for a show can have an impact on how you are perceived by the customers, so matching your outfit to the tastes of the crowd could increase sales.

For example, a boutique sponsored by the local social guild and held at a ritzy hotel, will draw women dressed in fashionable, expensive clothes. Wear your best, most sophisticated attire to such an event. Business expositions, held at large convention centers will draw an audience dressed in business suits and dresses. Choose conservative, traditional clothing for such events. Local country fairs are usually on the casual side, so sportswear would be appropriate. Just remember to consider your overall appearance when dressing for a show. It's always better to be overdressed, than dressed too casually. Pay careful attention to good hygiene and personal grooming, and no matter what style of dress you follow, wear comfortable shoes.

A Professional Attitude

Successful weekend entrepreneurs must convey a friendly and helpful attitude. To make money selling products or services at craft fairs and trade shows, vendors must enjoy dealing with people. Being pleasant to the customer is elementary, yet it is surprising how many vendors send out negative signals telegraphing their dislike for dealing with people.

To maintain a professional attitude, vendors also should be prepared to respond to unhappy customers occasionally. Decide in advance how you will handle returns or how you will deal with unpleasant crafters in the neighboring booth. Although unpleasant incidents are rare, you should anticipate them and consider what to do or say if they occur. Always be prepared to handle these situations calmly and diplomatically.

Happy customers can be the source of substantial referral business. So, give some thought to your return policy and how you will deal with an unsatisfied customer. Studies show that unhappy customers will tell twice as many friends negative things about a business as happy customers tell positive things. It's human nature for people to complain more than to compliment. Since complaints can kill sales quickly, plan your responses carefully.

Remember to be friendly, but not too aggressive; informative, but not pushy; enthusiastic, but not overbearing. Experience will help you find your best selling personality.

Using Body Language To Your Advantage

Studies show that men and women send out certain, strong messages just by the way they sit, stand or posture themselves. Standing with your arms crossed, for example, sends out a message to "keep your distance, don't come too close." Exhibitors can appear more approachable by keeping their arms at their sides or behind their back.

Making eye contact with potential customers projects warmth and friendliness. Try to catch the eye of all potential customers that come to your booth to look at your merchandise. Then, greet them with a smile and a simple, "hello" or "how are you doing, today?"

Avoid reading or occupying yourself with anything that does not pertain directly to your display or products. If you look too busy and don't acknowledge the customer's presence immediately, it is unlikely shoppers will approach you with questions. You will lose a chance to engage the prospect in conversation and qualify the person as a potential buyer.

On the other hand, do not look too idle, either. Busy yourself by straightening the stock or adding up receipts. Don't stand in your booth looking as if you are ready to pounce on the first person that shows the slightest interest.

Today's buyers are on guard, and most resent the overly aggressive salesperson. Successful selling begins when the vendor is able to tell the response and comfort level of the prospect by observing the shopper's body language.

Here is a simple technique you can use when the customer becomes uncomfortable as you approach the close of a sale. Take several steps backward or move away from the customer and busy yourself with something for a moment. Straighten your display, or put something into the waste basket. Watch the reactions of the customers and listen to their tone of voice. You will be amazed at how effective this gesture is for putting customers at ease and for letting them feel they are in control of the purchasing decision.

The study of body language has been the subject of many books and articles. Make some observations, read about the subject and incorporate what you learn in your selling methods. You will find applying this knowledge can make a difference in your sales effectiveness.

Your Sales Presentation

Think of selling as the art of persuasive conversation. Learning what to say, as well as how and when to say it, is the key to increasing your sales and profits. Effective selling is really very simple. Just remember the three E's of successful selling: **ENGAGE, EXCITE, ENCOURAGE.** You're probably thinking, "Sure, that sounds easy, but what exactly do I say?"

To start with, you cannot sit inside your booth patiently waiting for customers to come over and purchase your products. Some people actually believe their products will sell themselves. That's occasionally true, but research shows that initiating and following through with the proper selling process will generate many more sales.

Preparation is essential. To be comfortable with and capable at selling, you must be prepared. A sales presentation given by an accomplished salesperson generally follows a pattern. First, the salesperson approaches the prospect casually and starts a conversation with small talk. Then, the salesperson proceeds to gain the potential customer's confidence while informing them of the product's assets, in an unassuming manner. Through a series of questions and answers, the salesperson qualifies the prospect. Finally, the salesperson directs the customer to buy.

The sales presentation must be memorized and should vary from prospect to prospect only slightly. The best selling presentations are those that influence customers to buy, yet leave them pleased and satisfied that the decision to buy was their own.

Develop an effective presentation by writing down what you wish to say to each potential customer. Next, memorize the presentation word for word. Practice with your family and friends until you feel confident and comfortable with what you are saying. Lack of attention to the basics often is the reason many fail to succeed in sales. Stick to the presentation and use it consistently with all prospects.

A good salesperson must be attentive to the customer. This doesn't mean pouncing on everyone that comes within two feet of the display. It means keeping your eyes on their eyes. You are looking for the person who hesitates in front of your display, stares at your products from across the aisle, approaches with curiosity or stops to pick up an item. These cues indicate the customer wants to know more about the products.

When you notice these behaviors, it's time to make the critical first move to **ENGAGE** the prospect in a conversation and qualify the person as a potential buyer. Never start the conversation by saying, "May I help you?"

The automatic response usually is, "No thanks, just looking." Use what I call **"SHOPPER STOPPERS."** Shopper stoppers are special questions or statements that compel the customer to stay and talk with you. First, make eye contact, then say something like, "Hi, busy show isn't it?"

When politely responded to, you might say, "These T-shirts are 100% cotton and preshrunk."

Or, "I make these myself by sewing Italian lace to the bottoms of cotton T-shirts. What size were you looking for?"

Or, "How old is the child you have in mind for this outfit? We carry sizes one through toddler four."

Or, "These are machine washable, do you like the plain or flowered ones?"

Vendors selling handmade jewelry or custom-designed earrings might say, "I'll bet you've never seen anything like these new mother of pearl earrings before. Do you wear the pierced or the clip-on type?"

Or, "All our jewelry is handmade by Native Americans. This piece is from the Zuni tribe."

Or, "I carry both pierced and clip-on earrings. What color were you looking for?"

Vendors selling personal computers or laser printers offering a prize drawing at their booth, might say, "Did you register to win a new computer?"

When the prospect stops, the conversation would continue with, "What type of computer do you use now?"

Or, "This new model features a backlit screen and a modem, let me show you how great this works."

These are just a few examples of opening lines that attempt to **ENGAGE** customers and either make them stop and talk more, which indicates that a sale is possible, or force them to quickly answer and move on, which means they weren't interested and you saved yourself a lot of time.

Always remember exhibiting is done for the purpose of making sales. Be sure you have interested, qualified customers before you take up your time and their time giving a sales presentation. Many people will pass by your exhibit. In an eight-hour shift at a busy show, vendors will have an opportunity to talk to several hundred potential customers. If exhibitors spend time repeating their presentation to everyone, without thought to the prospect's financial ability to buy, timing, authority to purchase or desire for the products, they will wear themselves out and generate very few sales. Every person pursued should be a qualified buyer. With a little experience, potential customers can be spotted easily.

After the prospect has been qualified and shows continued interest, a successful salesperson moves on to step two, **EXCITE!** When appropriate, put the product in the customer's hands. Let them feel it, try it on or see how it works. Confirm that you have the right size, the right color and you can ship anywhere, if that's what it takes to make the sale. Offer information of interest that will create desire for your product. If you are selling something made by hand, tell the prospect how difficult it is to make, discuss the rarity of the materials used or the uniqueness of the design. A vender who is the artist, designer, inventor or crafter who made the item, should mention this to the prospect. Vendors merchandising the products of others can mention they are the exclusive distributor or the representative that travels to Hong Kong and personally selects each item. Enthusiasm sells, so take pride in your work and be a happy vendor.

Exhibitors representing a business product or personal service should demonstrate the benefits of their offerings. Show prospects what the service will do for them. Explain the extent of the warranty and tell why your product is better than others on the market. Indicate when delivery is possible, talk about quality and demonstrate performance.

When you feel prospects are convinced they need and want what you offer, proceed to step three. **ENCOURAGE** them to buy it, now. A simple, closing statement like, "May I wrap that up for you?" or "Let me show you our best payment schedule," will either result in the sale or bring up an objection. When potential customers present objections, they are saying "sell me more!"

The entire persuasive conversation or sales presentation takes only a matter of minutes. Here is an example of my sales presentation for personalized children's books.

A woman glances toward my display of books. I attempt to **ENGAGE** her with a **SHOPPER STOPPER.**

"Do you have a special little one to buy for?" The prospect nods yes and stops to get a closer look.

I open the book and hand it to her explaining, "Your favorite child is the star of the story. We customize each book right here in just four minutes."

The customer looks intrigued and asks, "What age group are these appropriate for?"

This is the time to **EXCITE** the prospect and continue to build interest. I explain, "They are perfect for children twelve years of age and under. Each book includes the child's name, age, city, family and friends in the story. How old is the child you have in mind?"

She replies, "My grandson is turning seven."

The customer is excited and qualified, so I attempt to **ENCOURAGE** her to buy now. "I recommend *The Lost Dinosaur*, little boys just love the story."

I hand her the selection and say, "All you need to do is fill out this form and I can make the book for you in four minutes."

The skilled salesperson always assumes the customer will buy, and behaves as if it's only a matter of time until the transaction takes place.

Why People Buy

There are two reasons why shoppers make purchases. First, because they are attracted to the product or service. The second reason, and many times the real reason the sale is made, is because the customer likes the vendor. Vendors who are always friendly, helpful and informative can influence how customers feel about their products. People enjoy buying from vendors who are excited about what they sell and who enjoy their work. Enthusiasm often can compensate for a lack of sales expertise.

In addition, shoppers often will buy a product simply because they discovered something in common with the vendor. To increase sales, always try to find a common bond with prospects. During a sales presentation you may discover you're both from the same hometown, your kids go to the same school, or you both have a Labrador Retriever. Believe it or not, these personal links often can be the reason a customer will buy from you, and not from your competitor. While trying to establish a link, never be too pushy or too talkative, and never get upset if you don't make the sale.

Overcoming Objections

Even if you are friendly and informative and able to give a great sales pitch, not every potential customer will be an easy sell. A person may hesitate to buy because an item is too expensive, too small, too large, not the right color, or a myriad of other reasons. These objections usually don't surface directly. Probe for objections throughout your conversation and listen for clues that will uncover the reasons shoppers are hesitating. When someone gives you an objection, remember they really are telling you "sell me more."

When you think you know what is preventing the prospect from making the purchase, confront him with it. If you think the problem is price, you might say, "I have several payment schedules available with no interest for six months. Which of these plans sound good to you?" The customer, at this point, might reveal the true problem. "I have to consult my partners first, before I make this purchase." If you think the problem is color or size and you can provide other choices not displayed, you might say "I can get these dresses in blue or yellow, too. Were you looking for a different color?" The customer, at this point, might reveal the true problem, like "My daughter has so many dresses, she really needs pants."

Learning to overcome objections is a very important part of your sales presentation. After developing your sales pitch, make a list of every excuse a customer might use for not purchasing your products or services. Next, write down what you will say as a rebuttal to each objection. Memorize your rebuttals and be prepared to use them when the customer presents an objection.

Sales professionals claim it takes six attempts to close a sale before the sale is made. The reason many people fail at sales is not because they can't sell, it's because they quit too soon. Wait until the customer gives you five no's. More than likely, your sixth try will close the sale.

Selling is an art. The more you learn about selling, the more you can earn for your business. Don't underestimate the need to acquire knowledge and expertise in selling. Read as many books on the subject as you can. Attend workshops and seminars to improve your skills. Observe and imitate other vendors who have excellent sales skills. The extra effort will pay off and help your weekend business grow and prosper.

Add-On Selling

The next time you eat at a fast food restaurant listen carefully to what the cashier says after you place an order. You probably will be asked if you would like an order of fries or a soft drink to go with your meal. This seemingly simple gesture is a calculated sales technique. It's one of the reasons why McDonald's is the leader in the fast food trade. All competitors now follow suit, but McDonald's pioneered the technique of the add-on sale. The goal of add-on selling is to get every customer to buy more than they originally intended.

By simply suggesting the customer might like a pair of colored laces to go with the new, hand-painted shoes or a computer dust jacket for the new laptop computer, a vendor may be able to increase the dollar amount of the sale substantially. Another way to encourage additional purchases is to offer a second item at a discount. When you are adding up the purchases at the register or writing out the sales receipt, mention a second item can be purchased at a discount off the regular price. Train yourself to always think in terms of add-on sales. Combine, match, pair or accessorize as many products as you can. You will be surprised how this will increase the dollar amount of each sale. Since you already have an interested customer, who is ready to make one purchase, it is easier to sell more to that customer than to start over with another one.

CHAPTER 9

LOW-COST PROMOTIONS FOR YOUR WEEKEND ENTERPRISE

Your weekend business and the products you sell will receive enormous exposure when you exhibit at trade shows and craft fairs. However, by using some creative advertising techniques and a few simple marketing concepts you can continue to generate business long after the event is over.

Cultivating satisfied customers will increase your sales and profits by providing repeat business and new customer referrals. The following promotional activities can be adapted to any exhibiting opportunity and can help establish a loyal customer following.

Business Cards

A business card can be the simplest and most effective business promotional tool an entrepreneur can use. In addition, business cards are cheap. Most communities have print shops that will produce 500, black and white business cards for under $20. Whether simple or fancy, business cards are a necessary tool for every weekend entrepreneur. Some business cards are more effective than others. So, pay attention to the suggestions that follow to help make your business card one of your best sales tools.

When you design your card, it should include your name, company name, address and phone number. If you work from home and don't wish to use your home address, get a post office box. If you are artistic, design a symbol or logo that represents your business and distinguishes your company from other businesses. If you cannot design such a symbol yourself, hire a professional graphic artist to design one for you, or check with a quick print shop, since many have low-cost, stock logos available. This symbol or logo should appear on all your advertising materials, since it will help create your business identity.

Your business card should do more than just identify your business; it also should work as an advertising tool. Include a memorable slogan or description that explains what you do or what you sell. This simple technique often is overlooked. When searching through my card file looking for a company that sells a particular product, I've come across dozens of cards reading Molly's Creations or Baker Enterprises. These cards never mention specifically what each company sells. Use business cards to explain what your business offers. For example, an exhibitor that sells office machines might put "Quality office machines and service" on the card. Or, simply list your products or services.

Don't be stingy with your cards. Give cards to business associates, customers and potential customers. Never be without your business cards; always carry them with you wherever you go. One marketing consultant said the only place an entrepreneur can be without a business card is in the shower. Business cards help customers remember you and they give you and your business credibility. So, never underestimate the importance of a good business card and be sure to give some thought and attention to the copy and the design of your cards. Some examples of excellent business cards follow:

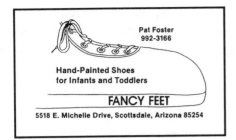

Hand Out Flyers Or Brochures

For stronger visual impact and more space for sales information, distribute flyers or brochures. Effective brochures and flyers provide detailed product information, a sales incentive and an order form for prospects that don't buy from you on the spot. Customers will be more likely to purchase your products after the show, if they have a reminder of what you offer and if you make ordering simple and convenient.

Before rushing off to the printer, put some thought into what you wish to accomplish with these advertising pieces. A flyer is usually an 8 1/2" x 11" sheet of paper with the message printed on one or both sides. An elaborate design is unnecessary, however, you should review the elements of effective print advertisements from books available in the library before you develop a flyer. Start with a catchy, attention-grabbing headline. For my personalized children's book business, I use the headline "Your favorite child is the star of the story!" on my flyers. The purpose of the strong headline is to entice people to continue reading and find out what is being offered. Take time to develop an attention-grabbing statement for your brochure or flyer.

Start by listing your products or services, explain discounts or deadlines for ordering, give prices including tax and postage, as well as payment options. Provide an order form indicating where to send the order. Photographs or drawings of your products on the flyer help remind the customer of exactly what you offer.

Printing your flyer with colored ink or using colored paper will increase the number of orders you receive. By shopping around, printers can be found that can do the job for $30-$40 per 1,000 copies. This price pertains to printing one color ink on white paper or black ink on colored paper. Printing on both sides will cost slightly more. Black ink on white paper is less expensive, costing $20-$30 per 1,000 copies.

Before spending money on expensive promotional literature, especially on a quality brochure, hire professional help or at least visit the library for information on advertising and brochure design. The cost of producing a quality brochure will be substantially more than the cost of a simple flyer. Your sales literature, however, will directly impact your business image. Therefore, make your flyers and brochures as professional looking as your budget will allow.

When participating in a show that draws thousands of people, vendors could give away thousands of flyers or brochures. If you've attended a trade show, you know how fast a sack can be filled with promotional literature. Some exhibitors practically force a brochure on everyone that passes by their booth. Many flyers, as well as expensive, four-color brochures get tossed away without being read.

To prevent your literature from ending up in the trash can, carefully select those who should receive it. Flyers are suitable for mass distribution, because they are relatively inexpensive to produce. An enterprise can be promoted with simple flyers costing about three cents each.

Expensive advertising literature should be distributed selectively. These pieces should be reserved for qualified prospects or potential customers to which you have given a sales presentation but did not make a sale. Effective brochures will continue to sell prospects on the benefits of your products or services long after they leave your booth. Also, give your best advertising piece to anyone that specifically asks for information about your product or services. Following these guidelines will alleviate the frustration of seeing your expensive brochures littering the parking lot outside the show site.

Order Forms

Brochures can be saved for new prospects, if you distribute order forms, instead of brochures, to your established customers. Since your customers are familiar already with your products, they simply need a reminder notice and an easy way to reorder. Order forms are less expensive to print than brochures or flyers, since they include only minimal sales information and pricing and you can print two forms per sheet of 8 1/2" x 11" paper. Always encourage repeat sales by placing an order form in the bag with each purchase.

Label All Products

Have a local printer make a roll of peel and stick labels imprinted with your company name, address and phone number. Place a label on the bottom, back or inside of all products. This will remind the customer where they can order more. The permanent label travels with the item, expanding your reach to customers taking the item out of town and out of state, encouraging additional sales. A legible label on the item makes it easy for the owner to purchase another by mail. Custom labels can be produced at most quick print shops or large office supply stores.

If you sell clothing, invest in custom, cloth labels that are sewn directly onto the garment. For your convenience, listed below are several companies that manufacture them.

Bach Label Company, 1212 S. San Pedro St., Los Angeles, CA 90015, 1-800-522-3563.

Newark Dressmaking Supply, 6473 Ruch Rd., P.O. Box 2448, Lehigh Valley, PA 18001.

North West Tag & Label, 110 Foothills Rd., Lake Oswego, OR 97034, (503) 636-6456.

Contests And Drawings

Sales leads for potential customers can be accumulated easily by having everyone that visits your booth leave a business card or fill out a contest form that will enter them into a prize drawing. The contest form should request the entrant's name, address and phone number. Have a box, basket or bowl close by where the forms or business cards can be deposited.

Select a prize from your inventory to be awarded at the end of the show and display it prominently at your booth. By giving away one of your products or services, you will know those entering the drawing are interested in what you offer. The purpose of the drawing isn't to collect as many names as possible, it's to obtain as many qualified leads as possible.

Spinning a wheel of chance for a free insurance evaluation, or guessing the number of jelly beans in a jar for a chance to win a free floral wreath are examples of games and contests commonly used at shows. Any activity that encourages audience participation, like pushing a button or turning a dial, works to gain attention and attract people to an exhibit booth. This approach is different from a drawing, but the goal is the same....to generate leads.

If a contest will be the focal point of your display, encourage everyone that seems qualified to fill out a form and take a chance. Make sure you follow up with these leads after the show by soliciting sales from the entrants by mail or phone. Many unqualified prospects will be on this list, so expect only a small number of actual sales from this advertising method.

Premium Giveaways

Advertising specialty items like key chains, balloons, pens, buttons, and magnets that have your company name and phone number on them make excellent giveaway items. A friend of mine, who sells advertising specialties, refers to them as the gift that "remains to be seen." Customers love to receive them and they serve to remind everyone about your business. You can find dealers offering these items in the Yellow Pages under the heading "Advertising Specialties."

Donate Gifts

Many local charities and organizations hold fundraising events and auctions throughout the year. These organizations always are looking for companies willing to donate items and gift certificates to support these events. In return for a donation, the supplier usually receives a free mention in the event program providing excellent exposure for a company and its products.

This method of free advertising can increase a company's visibility, strengthen credibility within the community and make the vendor feel good, too. Look for a list of upcoming charitable events in the leisure section of your local paper, then call and offer a door prize or auction item.

Use Hang Tags

When a permanent, stick-on label is not practical for your product, design a tag you can attach with a string or safety pin. Along with your business name, address, phone number and company logo, add something creative to the tag. Print washing instructions, provide product history, list ingredients, or add an interesting tidbit about the artist or designer that will stick in the buyer's mind or make the buyer keep the tag.

Demonstrate Your Wares

Demonstrations almost always attract crowds. They create excitement and can catch the attention of shoppers passing an exhibit. To prove a point, consider events that have featured an artist drawing caricatures of shoppers. The area around the artist is swarming with people eager to see what's going on.

Demonstrations have been used as a successful sales promotion method by artists, sculptors, wood carvers, potters and glass blowers. Demonstrations also have worked for chiropractors, computer suppliers, coffee vendors and image consultants. A selling advantage is obtained if you can show how a product is made, how a product works, or how it feels, smells or tastes. Windmills, wooden toys, computer generated products, balsa airplanes, sculptured nails, skin care products and computers are examples of products that can be demonstrated effectively at craft fairs or trade shows. The more senses you can bring into play to stimulate the potential buyer, the more impact your product will have.

Informal demonstrating can be done throughout the day at the booth. Many trade shows also have a designated area for demonstrations, with appropriate seating that is designed to accommodate a crowd. Promoters advertise the demonstrations over the loud speaker and print a schedule listing demonstrations in the program handed out to people attending the show. Always inquire about the availability of a demonstration area. If you can utilize this extra promotional opportunity to demonstrate your products or services, make a request to be included in the schedule.

For products not easily demonstrated at the booth, consider using communication technology to show how it works or how it was made. For example, a small TV monitor can be placed at the front of your display with a repeating, 90-second videotape of the manufacturing process. Another interesting approach is to make a model showing your product in various stages of construction. A story board of photographs could show the same thing. Any of these methods can show how your product is used. Use your imagination, and you will sell more. In addition, time passes quicker when vendors are busy demonstrating their wares.

Hire Personalities

With a larger budget for promotion, an exhibitor can draw a crowd to a display by hiring either a human or imaginary celebrity. The type of celebrity should tie-in with the exhibitor's business or with the event's theme. When the objective is to attract large numbers of people to the exhibit, vendors can hire a Ninja Turtle, Smokey the Bear, a face-painting clown, a politician, a sports star or a movie star look-a-like. These personalities can sign autographs, model products or just hang around the booth to attract customers. Be sure to let the local media know about the celebrity promotion, since the effort may result in seeing your booth featured on the evening news or in the morning newspaper. Always mention your attraction in all your advertising and promotional activities prior to the show. Be prepared for a deluge of curiosity seekers. You will need to work hard to find the qualified prospects, but if nothing else, your products will be noticed. With this approach, it is wise to bring extra help to assist with sales and crowd control.

Teach Your Talents

Good speakers and instructors are always in demand by civic and community groups and local colleges. If you enjoy talking to people and are willing to share your expertise with others, many schools, clubs and organizations would love to have you address their members and students.

Volunteering time to speak to interested groups or to teach your craft, can give you credibility and recognition as an expert in your field. Occasionally you may be paid for your presentation, but more often the payback comes in the form of publicity, contacts and sales of your products.

Whenever you address a group, bring your flyers or brochures to distribute. Pass around an attendance sheet and ask for the names and addresses of those who wish to be on your mailing list. In most cases, it's not appropriate to do any direct selling in your role as teacher or presenter, but you should make your products and services known to the audience.

To announce your availability as a speaker, call local colleges, and request an application to teach non-credit courses. Join a speaker's bureau at the local Chamber of Commerce or call the parks and recreation department or YMCA. These organizations always are looking for new and interesting instructors.

Networking

One of the best ways to get additional exposure for your business is to become involved in community organizations. Join trade organizations or clubs appropriate to your business first, since you will benefit from meeting others with similar interests. Organizations that provide excellent networking opportunities include the Chambers of Commerce, leads groups, Rotary, Toastmasters, Entrepreneur's clubs and business groups.

These professional, business and support groups hold meetings regularly and provide a forum for meeting interesting people, making business contacts, exchanging business cards and generating leads for future business. Some organizations provide members with the opportunity to give a 30-second commercial to tell about products and services or to make a business announcement.

Involvement in community organizations can help entrepreneurs build a vast network of contacts and resources, as well as gain information that will be useful in the future. So, go out there and get involved, it's good for business.

Seek Free Publicity

What is publicity? Publicity is free advertising disguised as a news story. A feature article in the daily newspaper about you and your business can generate extraordinary interest in what you do and what you sell. Exposure through the news media can really boost sales, as well as establish business credibility.

Publicity has two big advantages over advertising. First, publicity is more credible to the public, because it is perceived as news, something of interest or something important. Second, the business does not pay for the print space or broadcast airtime. Obtaining publicity, however, takes time and effort. Contacting reporters about your business and enticing them to write a story can be time consuming and sometimes frustrating.

To get your business in the news, you must develop an "angle", a unique slant to your story that offers the media something special or different to report. Your "angle" must be newsworthy, provide human interest or tie into a current trend or topic. For example, I obtained four feature articles with photos about my business in Arizona newspapers when I mentioned to reporters that I was a career woman turned entrepreneur after the birth of my son. This topic, the woman on the career track switching to the mommy track, then to the entrepreneur track, was my angle. It was a timely topic of interest for many readers of the newspapers that published the articles and the journalists were happy to report it.

Newsworthy topics include receiving an award, holding a contest, sponsoring an event, introducing a new product, writing a book, teaching a seminar or expanding the company. The information you give the media must educate, enlighten, amuse or inform the general public. It also must be timely. Always send publicity information to the media at least two weeks in advance of an event, to meet deadlines for weekly publications. The newspapers cannot help publicize your event if you don't supply the information prior to their deadlines.

Once you decide on an angle for your story, plan your approach for contacting the media. Contact the small, community papers first. You can make a few mistakes learning the ropes with these publications without ruining your chances for placing a story.

Start by placing a phone call. If you have a business angle, call the newspaper and ask to speak to the business editor. If your angle is of general interest to the readers, ask for the features editor. Tell the editor you would like to discuss a story idea. Explain your story, using your "angle" to interest the editor in assigning a reporter. Be sure not to pitch your product or services directly. When a pitch is too commercial, the editor will take offense and tell you to contact the advertising department about buying ad space. If your idea is appealing, editors will request additional information in writing or schedule an interview immediately.

When the media requests written information about a story idea, the standard format used to respond is a new release. Each release competes with hundreds of other releases, so it must be both intriguing and concise in order to gain attention. A well-written news release should begin with an attention-grabbing headline, followed by a paragraph that answers the questions who, what, when, where, why and how, as it pertains to your product, service, event or business. Examine every detail about your business to determine what you might have to offer the media.

WHO? Who are you in the community? Who benefits from your products or services? Who do you know that might have an impact on your appeal to the media? Who should attend the event you are planning?

WHAT? What do you do? What is your product or service? What event are you involved with? What can you teach someone? What have you achieved or invented? What difficulties have you faced? What have you overcome to get where you are?

WHEN? When did you get started? When will your products be available? When should the information be released? When does the offer expire? When does the event take place?

WHERE? Where can your products be found? Where are you from? Where were you educated? Where did you learn what you do? Where do your products come from?

WHY? Why should anyone be interested in what you do or sell? Why did you pursue this business venture? Why does anyone need what you have? Why do you want the public to know this information?

HOW? How did you get started? How can someone benefit from your offerings? How can someone get what you're offering? How does it work? How good is it? How do you make it?

Use the standard format when composing your news release. Type, double spaced, all the information on one side of an 8 1/2" x 11" sheet of paper. Include the words FOR IMMEDIATE RELEASE in the top left corner, skip down three spaces then put CONTACT: followed by your name, address and phone number. Skip down a few spaces then type your headline followed by a paragraph that answers who, what, when where, why and how. Reporters are under strict space and time constraints, so express your ideas and information plainly, concisely and in as short a space as possible. Present the information in descending order of importance. If the editor must review hundreds of releases, you must present the most important information in the first paragraphs, since the last half of a release may never be read. Information in the first paragraph should sum up the complete idea of the story angle.

After sending the information to the reporter, wait a week, and follow up with a phone call. Inquire whether the information was received and if there are any questions concerning the facts. You'll get an indication from the conversation whether the reporter is interested in pursuing the story further. Don't hesitate to ask if there is an interest in the idea. If turned down, approach again in a few months with a slightly different angle.

Publicity can have a beneficial impact on your business. The time and trouble it takes to cultivate publicity is well worth the effort. If you feel unable to handle this task by yourself, hire a professional public relations firm to help you.

Develop A Mailing List

Begin accumulating names for mailing lists immediately, categorizing them by letters "A" and "B". The "A" list should contain the name, mailing address and phone number of every buying customer. A good mailing list is a valuable commodity and important for business growth. In addition, companies listed in the Yellow Pages under "mailing lists" may be willing to buy or rent names on your list, thus providing additional income.

To establish an "A" list, start by copying the information found on every check received as payment for a purchase. Better yet, use a receipt book or duplicate invoice for every sale and record customer information at the top. A list of customers who know and appreciate your products or your company's service is a valuable, money-making tool.

Another mailing list to develop, but keep separate from the "A" list, is a list of prospects. Interested prospects who have not yet made a purchase will comprise your "B" list. Obtain names for the "B" list from the entry forms submitted for door prize drawings, names you collect from networking activities and referrals from existing customers. Your "B" list represents potential sales and needs a special advertising piece to solicit business. The goal is to see how many names on the "B" list of prospects you can move to the "A" list of customers.

What To Send In A Mailing

Mail to your "A" list twice a year. The first mailing should be completed immediately after the holiday season and mail again in September or October. Many benefits are derived from regular correspondence with your customers, not the least of which is additional sales. Develop a customer mailing piece that includes some of the following suggestions.

Thank customers for their business. Let customers know you appreciate their support and patronage. This gesture promotes good will and strengthens customer loyalty.

Introduce a new product. Let your customers be the first to learn about a new product and offer them a special preferred customer discount. This usually will generate an instant rush of orders.

Announce an event. Use a special occasion to communicate with customers about exciting things happening within your business. An anniversary, new location, or an invitation to an open house are occasions that give you a reason to contact customers. Offer a special sale or discount.

Send sales literature. Include a separate coupon for a discount on the next purchase. Always print a 30-day expiration date on the coupon to encourage an immediate response. Announce a special sale for preferred customers only.

Take a survey. Uncover customer needs, opinions and complaints about your products or the way you do business. You can put this information to use managing your enterprise. Ask customers to rate your services, products, quality, prices, delivery time or return policy on a scale from one to 10. Ask for suggestions on improving your business or what new services or products customers would like to see added to your line. Your customers will appreciate the fact that you value their opinions and patronage. Simple, do-it-yourself market research can help you focus on your customer's needs, identify your company's strengths and weaknesses, and help to make sound business decisions.

Solicit testimonials. Ask customers what they like best about what you do or sell. Find out how others react to your products. Ask if your products live up to their expectations. When you receive favorable responses from your most satisfied customers, ask for permission to quote them in your advertising.

Ask for referrals. Do not overlook this simple method for obtaining new business leads. The best form of advertising has always been word-of-mouth. Reward your customers with a gift or discount if they provide you with the names and mailing addresses of friends that might like to receive your sales information.

Send publicity reprints. When your business or products receive publicity coverage in a local magazine or newspaper, clip the article, make copies and send these to your customers along with other sales materials.

Include your show schedule. Keep customers informed about where you will be exhibiting in the future. Provide customers with a copy of your show schedule. One effective way to do this is to copy the schedule onto the front or back of a publicity reprint described above.

Update Your Mailing Lists

If you send your mailing first class, be sure to use envelopes with a return address on them. After each mailing, the post office will automatically return all the letters that were not delivered with the corrected information for you to update the mailing list. Keeping your mailing list up to date and free of duplications or incorrect addresses will save postage.

Save On Postage

You can cut your postage costs one-third by co-oping your mailing. This means finding two other businesses that sell complementary, but non-competing products to a similar customer base and offering to let them "piggy back" their sales literature in your envelope. You can mail four, 8 1/2" x 11" flyers in a #10 envelope for the price of one first-class stamp. Each participating business pays one-third of the postage expense plus the cost of a flyer. Everyone benefits from such an economical approach. As your business grows and your mailing list numbers more than 200 customers, explore the benefits of obtaining a bulk rate permit to further reduce postage expenses.

CHAPTER 10

HELPFUL RESOURCES

Starting a business can seem overwhelming. Where do you find display materials, office supplies or business assistance? Many people are not aware of the help that is available in their own communities. This chapter includes some of the sources and suppliers that may be beneficial to your weekend enterprise.

Business Assistance

U.S. Small Business Administration (SBA) ,1441 L. Street N.W.,Washington D.C. 20416. 1-800-368-5855 .

Ask for a list of SBA publications and video tapes about starting and managing a business. Most are free.

Small Business Development Centers (SBDC)

Look in the Yellow Pages for the local SBDC in your area. A branch of the SBA, this agency provides free counseling, a resource center and seminars on subjects like marketing, bookkeeping, financing, customer relations, home business management and computer systems for small business owners.

Service Core of Retired Executives (SCORE), 655 15th Street N.W., Suite 901, Washington, DC 20005-5742.

A branch of the SBA, this agency is made up of 13,000 retired business owners and managers who volunteer their knowledge and expertise to assist small business owners with confidential counseling and low-cost seminars.

Internal Revenue Service/State Departments of Revenue

The IRS provides a free business owner's kit that contains valuable information on tax and licensing requirements for start-up companies. Plus, contact the Department of Revenue in your state and the City Treasury in any cities where you plan to exhibit for sales tax information and vendor's licenses.

Public Libraries - Don't forget your public library as a resource. Librarians can help you find answers to almost any question. Business directories, media guides and business how-to books are all available at the library.

Networking Organizations

Entrepreneurial Mothers Association (EMA), P.O. Box 2561, Mese, Arizona 85204.

Arizona-based business and support group offering networking opportunities and educational information for self-employed mothers.

National Association of Women Business Owners (NAWBO), 600 South Federal Street, Suite 400, Chicago, Illinois 60605. (1-800) 272-2000

The largest professional organization for women business owners. Local chapters provide educational programs, networking and business advocacy activities.

Mother's Home Business Network (MHBN), P.O. Box 423, East Meadow, New York 11554. (516) 997-7394

An informative newsletter and networking tool for more than 30,000 home-based businesses nationwide.

The Chamber of Commerce of the U.S., 1615 H St., NW, Washington, DC 20062. (202) 659-6000

The Small Business Programs Office acts as a central clearinghouse for information on everything from getting started in business to expanding your business overseas. Check in your telephone directory for the nearest Chamber of Commerce in your area.

The National Federation of Independent Business, 600 Maryland Ave., SW, Suite 700, Washington DC 20024. (202) 554-900

American Entrepreneurs Association, 2392 Morris Ave., Irvine, CA 92714. (714) 261-2325

National Association of Entrepreneurs, 2378 S. Broadway, Denver, CO 80210. (303) 426-1166

Professional Trade Show Displays

Check in the Yellow Pages for dealers or manufacturers in your area. Also, your local librarian can help you locate other companies that specialize in displays, fixtures and supplies.

ShowTopper Exhibits, The Godfrey Group, P.O. Box 10247, Raleigh, NC 27605-9990. (919) 544-6504

Nomadic Instand, P.O. Box 9113, Cathedral Station, Boston, MA 02118. (1-800) 848-4400

Professional Displays, Inc., 738 Arrowgrand Circle, Covina, CA 91722. (1-800) 222-6838

Skyline Displays, 3421 E. Wood Street, Phoenix, Arizona 85040. (1-800) 328-2725

AAA Display, 1313 E. Barbara Drive, Tempe, AZ 85281. (1-800) 658-9196

Visual Marketing Products, 2005 E. University, Phoenix, AZ 85034. (602) 256-6687

Display Fixtures And Supplies

Siegel Display Products, P.O. Box 95, Minneapolis, MN 55440. (612) 340-1493

Merchandise Presentation, Inc., 3960 Merritt Avenue, Bronx, NY 10466

Jay Display and Fixture Corporation, 1045 10th Avenue, San Diego, CA 92101

The Nu-Era Group, Inc., 727 North Eleventh Street, Saint Louis, MO 63101. (1-800) 325-7043

Crafter's Malls

Coomer's The Crafter's Mall, 6012 Reefs Point Lane Suite F, Ft. Worth, TX 76135. (1-800) 922-4588

Arizona Art and Crafts Market, 4750 North 16th Street, Phoenix, AZ 85016 . (602) 248-7090

Canopies & Tents

Sam's Quick Canopies, 52700 US 131 North, Three Rivers, MI 49093. (616) 273-3425.

Shade Canopies, Rt. 4, Box 480C-2, Clearborne, TX 76031. (1-800) 323-3209

Swap Meets

SwapMart, 5115 North 27th Avenue, Phoenix, AZ 85017. (602) 246-9600 Festival Markets Inc., of Las Vegas operates these indoor swap meets for vendors with new merchandise and has similar facilities in Las Vegas, NV and Tucson, AZ.

Swap Meets West, 295 N. Broadway #147, Santa Maria, CA 93455. (805) 928-2205. Newsletters, guides and information on swap meets in California.

The Great American Flea Market Directory, P.O. Box 543, Fenton, MO 63026. A national directory of flea markets, swap meets, trade days and dealer auctions.

The Merchandiser Group's Guide, Sumner Communications, 72 North Street, Suite 201, Danbury, CT 06810. (203) 748-2050. A national directory of active, operating, predominately new merchandise markets across the United States.

INDEX